Go Motorhoming Europe

GEORGE DOREE

Published by Vicarious Books LLP, PO Box 72, Minehead, Somerset, TA24 9AL www.vicariousbooks.co.uk Registered Office, Nash House, Swain Street, Watchet, Somerset TA23 0AB

First published 2006

ISBN 0-9552808-0-X 978-0-9552808-0-1

Printed in the UK by 4edge Limited - www.4edge.co.uk

Dedicated to Laurie who instead of saying 'he'd do it next year' did it this year. Unfortunately there wasn't a next year.

About the Authors

Chris Doree and Meli George have always been around the camping and caravan scene. Chris's family's love for fishing and the great outdoors provided many nights under canvas and he bought his first caravan at the tender age of 27. Meli is third generation, her grandfather having built his own caravan in true post war fashion. Family holidays were enjoyed both under canvas and in various touring caravans. They met during a humanitarian aid convoy to Kosovo, Meli driving a converted transit and Chris an HGV. Whilst sat at Bari docks, Southern Italy, they dreamt of a grand tour. Two caravans, two motorhomes and 18 months of intense research later, they set off to see the sights and seek a new life.

Their motorhome enabled them to experience winter, summer and midnight sun, skiing and touring. They travelled throughout Europe, including non-EU member states, resting at campsites, camper-stops and free-parks. Temperatures had a 58°C range from minus 21°C to plus 37°C. They have full time toured for 14 months. They have stayed static on site for six months. They have literally been from one extreme to another.

Motorhoming opened up a world of opportunities; from judging grappa competitions, to finding deserted thermal waters, beaches and fjords; it changed their lives forever.

They have owned the following vehicles:

- Gulf Stream, Sun Sport a 27" long American A-class, towing a fiat Cinquecento.
- Mazda Bongo Japanese import B-class 4x4 with elevating roof.
- Hymer B654 self imported German A class, towing an Aixam micro car.
- Home conversion transit van, used for humanitarian aid runs to Kosovo and Ukraine.
- Lunar Eclipse caravan, fulltime wintering in England.
- Various caravans of all ages and berths
- Swift Sundance C-class (at the time of writing)

Acknowledgements

We are very grateful to people who have given up their time to help us. We would like to thank Paul George for his excellent illustrations, editorial advice and years of fatherly encouragement. We are very grateful to Colin & Margaret Varney and David & Jane Asplin for their editorial advice and support. Our appreciation goes to John Wickersham for his advice at short notice.

Many thanks are extended to friends and family who have tolerated our sudden appearances and unusual requests during these years.

To all the people we met along the way we would like to say 'thank you', for letting us in your motorhomes, answering our questions, information sharing and for providing us with such good company.

To the many strangers who helped us, thank you for your assistance and for restoring our faith in human kindness.

Cat
© paulgeorge 06

Foreword

This book aims to provide definitive answers for people motorhoming in Europe, whether first time or full time motorhomers. Detailed within each section are a series of possibilities, providing sound advice, and identifying sources of quality information. The content of this book is formed from our own experience and research. The views expressed are our own personal opinion because there is no 'right' way; just what's right for you.

Every endeavour has been made to ensure that the information is as accurate as possible at the time of publication. Unfortunately the world stands still for no one so the reader should confirm the legality or safety of any undertaking. All advice is followed at the individual's own risk and no responsibility is accepted by the authors or publishers for any loss, damage, injury or inconvenience whatsoever, howsoever caused to anyone using this book.

Over to you

We intend, when timely, to update this edition. Between editions things will change so we would be very grateful if readers could inform us of any changes or developments. We will endeavor to put updated information on www.go-motorhoming.co.uk. In addition if you have further questions please contact us via the website, alternatively send a SAE with your questions to PO Box 72 Minehead, Somerset TA 24 9AL. We reserve the right to publish excerpts from correspondences and will acknowledge your name unless you clearly state otherwise.

Contents

Introduction

Many of us dream of enjoying periods of European culture and climate, from annual holidays to grand tours, winter pilgrimage or seeking a long-term solution.
Europe is the playground of motorhomes. Campsites are everywhere. Many countries have camper-stops or the privilege to free-park. Knowledge is power. This publication empowers its readers, enabling them to enjoy the best motorhoming experience possible. This book is aimed at everyone, no matter what their budget or dream. It provides information to guide people through the realities of visiting Europe. Whether you intend to Campervan, Motorcaravan, Recreational Vehicle (RV), or Camping Car, these come under the umbrella of the title 'Motorhome'. Although aimed at motorhomers it has equally relevant information for caravanners.

Throughout the book further information is identified, including 203 internet addresses. This is due to the lack of printed information and convenience, web pages can be saved and re-accessed whilst travelling or viewed live on the Internet. Where available, contact details are listed in the back of the book.
This book is laid out in sections for easy use and reference. We recommend that you read from cover to cover to gain the whole picture. Useful information is distributed throughout.

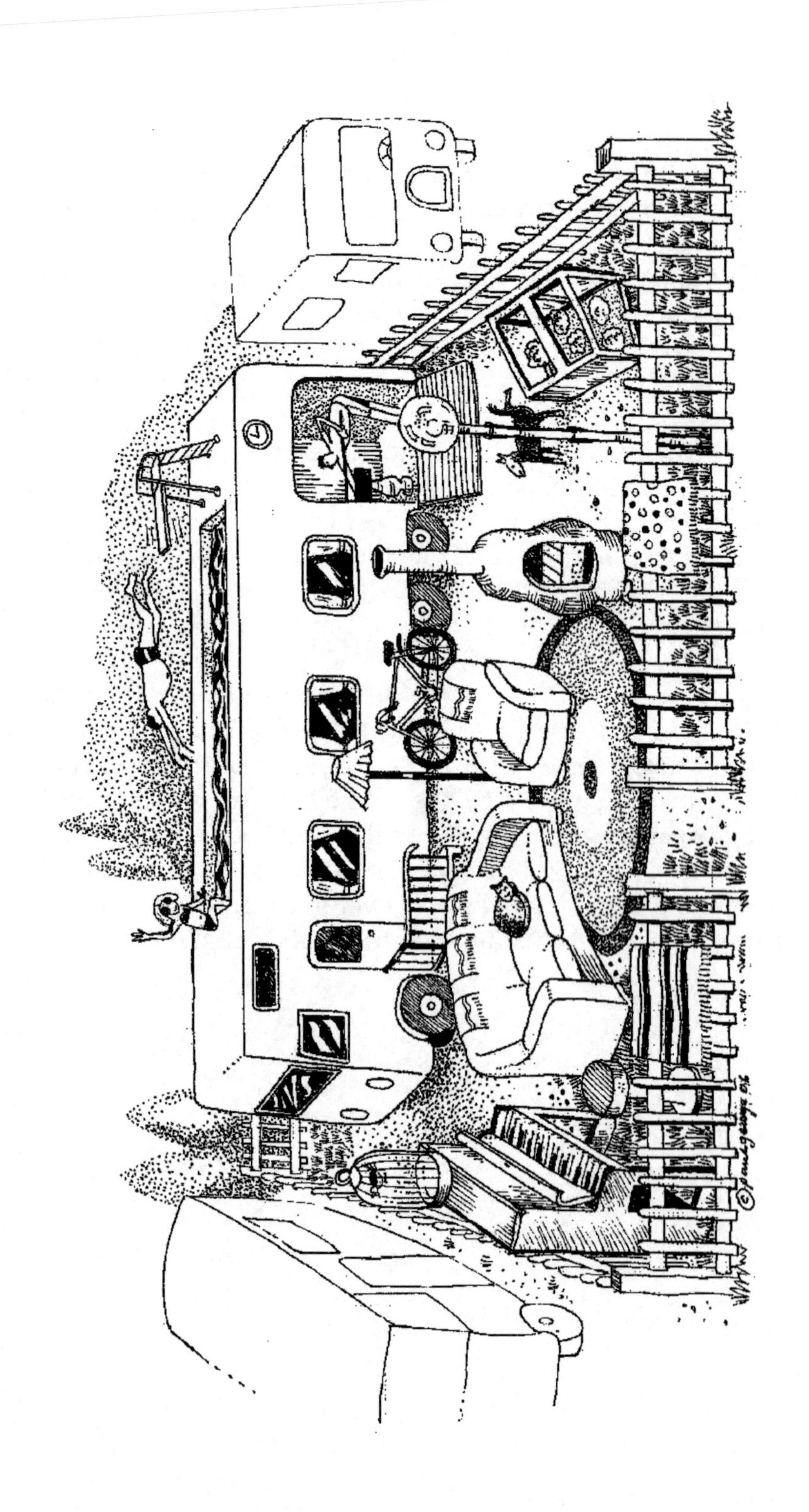

Chapter 1 - First Time or Full Time

The Motorhome - a car, a house, an escape; no wonder you've always wanted one - the retirement present you worked so hard for, to see the sights or enjoy Mediterranean winters. A vehicle suitable for a grand tour or alternative lifestyle, a practical and economical option for those with limited budgets or the restraints of return flights home. The perfect transport to find a new life abroad, or the enabler for thousands of hobbyists whilst following their passion. An extreme vehicle to go where no man has been before, or simply your day-to-day vehicle used for pleasant week-ends and holidays. Whatever your calling, the motorhome offers the freedom and spontaneity unrivalled by any other means of travel, always with that reassuring home from home feeling, wherever you find yourself.

Motorhomes appeal in as many different ways as there are people wanting one, therefore no 'one fits all' option is possible. When the motorhome and situation are compatible they are an excellent tool, providing unrivalled freedom and excellent after purchase economy. Identifying what type(s) of motorhomer you are will enable you to take full advantage of this wonderful resource. Failing to identify your motorhoming requirements could lead to a stressful, un-enjoyable and expensive experience.

This book provides qualified answers for everyone, detailing, how, when and where to motorhome in Europe.

First time

You would not purchase a car without test driving it and you are unlikely to test drive a car you know is unsuitable. After all you already know the concept, so you know whether you want a Porsche or a Panda. The old adage 'buy in haste repent at leisure' could not be more accurate when it comes to motorhomes.

Hiring or better still borrowing a motorhome, especially if you have not owned a touring caravan, is highly recommended. Many escorted holidays provide a hire option so all the hard work is done. These holidays have experienced people on hand to show you the ropes and give advice on all your questions. Hire costs may seem expensive but will almost certainly save you money in the long run, and the experience will probably cause you to choose a completely different motorhome than you originally thought. Some hire companies offer special purchase deals post hire.

As with any luxury purchase it takes time to find out how frequently you use it, if at all, and whether a sensible purchase was made.

Our first motorhome a 27' (8.23m) American was purchased with our grand tour in mind. We thought it was fantastic, the common consensus at the time agreed it was ideal for visiting Europe. We joined the American motorhome clubs and attended their organised rallies. Although it answered our every living space desire, spontaneity was seriously reduced. It was difficult to park in towns or drive down country lanes. Not all UK campsites, especially smaller farm style sites, have suitable pitches, entrances or approaches. We hated having to phone round campsites, only to discover their nervousness over accessibility. This lack of mobility proved too much of a compromise. We down sized to a 6.5m (21'4") European motorhome, proving comfortable for two. The compromise on the living space was worth it for the manoeuvrability and running costs. We now own a 5.25m (17"3') British motorhome with a perfectly adequate layout for long-term use.

An equally viable option is to buy a budget motorhome, which has reached the point where depreciation is entirely down to condition. Therefore if used sympathetically for a short time there should be little difference between purchase and sale price. This is a great way to find out what you must have but more importantly what you can do without. Buy carefully and you will have no problem reselling. See ***Chapter 2*** for a full explanation.

We eventually took our own advice and hired a narrow boat whilst writing this book. Having had a fantastic fortnight we can definitely say that we are not going to own one, but will "navigate the cut" again one day. If you too have enjoyed boating on the inland waterways then you are likely to enjoy the freedom of motorhome travel. Boaters predominantly stop overnight anywhere they fancy as long as there's no restriction, this is just like free-parking or using camper-stops and a good way to get over any nerves you may have.

Further Information

A list of hire companies can be found at the Practical Motorhome website www.practicalmotorhome.co.uk or at the back of motorhome magazines.

The Motorhome for Holidays

Many motorhomes are viable primary or secondary vehicles. All provide the opportunity for weekends and holidays, with the option to visit the continent on a whim. Parties and pubs can be enjoyed where overnight parking permits.

On a shoe-string

Being limited by budget or visas is no problem, as a motorhome does provide cheap, efficient, flexible travel to multiple countries, providing freedom to go anywhere without the inconvenience of public transport, or the endless search for accommodation and sustenance. By using camper-stops and free-parking, Europe can be very cheap and you don't have to carry your world on your back. In London, campervan style motorhomes are advertised in local newspapers, youth hostels, or sold direct at Market St, N1. Those who make a wise purchase and use the motorhome sympathetically should achieve the same resale price. Good purchases and bad sales can be made when foreign nationals do not leave enough time before return flights home.

In Italy we met two South Africans touring in a hardtop pickup. They were struggling with their budget. They had a tent but no fridge or practical cooking facilities. They couldn't use free camper-stops, making their trip more expensive and less enjoyable. Ironically Italy has the most expensive campsites and some of the best camper-stops. A reasonable motorhome could have been purchased for the same amount as their pickup.

Holiday Home

A motorhome offers the benefits of a holiday home, but the freedom to move and change scenery on a whim. Some campsite users stay up to six months, whilst others leave their leisure vehicle permanently sited. Campsites offer season pitches, or the option to purchase on a 99-year lease. Cheap flights and ferries make it is perfectly feasible to use your leisure vehicle as a holiday home. It is advisable, if possible, to stop at the chosen campsite for an extended period prior to any commitments being made.

Those intending to buy and live on a pitch full time will find American style motorhomes are both suited and very popular. Their comfortable living space, air conditioning and under floor lockers are excellent. A large caravan, or an American style articulated pickup truck and trailer (fifth wheel) would work equally well for a considerably lower price.

Thousands of Brits spend cheap winters on Iberian campsites. These cater very well for this market, having regular events, activities and transport. As there is little on offer outside of Iberia, many return year after year, forming strong communities. Most British motorhome clubs organise winter rallies. Independently booking a campsite is common.

Further Information

Mountain View is a series of parks being built. The pitches can be purchased on 99-year lease. Visit www.mountainparkview.com Tel: 01293 545577

The Fifth Wheel Company, Denbighshire based manufacturer of very good fifth wheels www.fifthwheelco.com Tel: 01745 583000.

MCL (another Welsh company) custom build heavy commercial vehicle based luxury motorhomes www.mcl-motorhomes.com Tel: 01766 770011.

Many campsites advertise long stays in the rear of magazines.

Adventure Tours

Don't think that motorhoming is all about campsites and meanders through the French countryside. The motorhome provides the opportunity to flex your adventure muscle. The frontier extends annually pushing further into Eastern Europe and Northern Africa. Some see Europe as the gateway to the Middle East and Asia.

There are clubs that help with planning for independent expeditions, and specialist companies that organise escorted tours, with varied durations to a variety of countries.

Further Information

Visit www.silkroute.org.uk for a group that helps organise and assist tours to China and other countries on the Silk Route. Membership to the Silk Route club costs £35.

www.xor.org.uk is an excellent website detailing which vehicle to take, what to pack and personal accounts of tours with useful links to other websites.

www.go-overland.com also has a wealth of information for extreme overland trips

www.first48.com is a company offering tours and has specially converted vehicles you can hire

www.chinaexploration.com specialises in tours of China either in your own vehicle or a hired one.

The Motorhome as an Aid (tool)

House Hunting

If you intend to move whether home or abroad, a motorhome reconnaissance is an excellent way to evaluate a country and choose a community. Locating a suitable house from home can be very difficult, and your expectations will rarely be met in reality. During the hunt a motorhome is convenient and affordable. The vast number of campsites across Europe, and the goodwill of local people, allows integrated access into a chosen community. Staying and getting a feel for it is beneficial beyond belief. If you buy a property requiring renovation the motorhome then provides somewhere to live.

Having sold our house and possessions, we left Britain looking for a new life in Europe. We were sure it would be Italy. Having spent two and a half months touring the country, we were surprised at not having found somewhere we wanted to live. We fell in love with Sicily but after a month realised it was not suitable. We then considered Greece and scoured Bulgaria, only to discover there's no place like home. If we had purchased over the Internet, as we were tempted to do, we would have been committed.

Further Information

The TV series 'A Place in the Sun' has an accompanying book. Information on purchasing a property abroad is detailed. Also magazines on individual countries are for sale at newsagents.

The Hobbyist - Eventer

Whatever your hobby, artists and windsurfers alike, can take advantage of motorhome freedom. Unrestrained by convention, the limitations are endless, providing cheap and convenient accommodation unrestricted by tour operators. Those with heavy equipment need to read the payload section in this book as most motorhomes have only sufficient weight capacity for passengers and limited luggage.

Motorhomes are suitable winter sports accommodation. Only those designed to cope with very low temperatures, should be used in the coldest periods. These motorhomes are described as "winterised" and have the following features: thicker insulation, double glazed windows, integral water and waste tanks and a large output blown air heater, ducted around the entire motorhome, including lockers to ensure pipes do not freeze.

We always intended to go skiing and purchased an appropriately winterised motorhome. We left the warmth of Greece behind starting the ski season on New Year's Day in Bulgaria. With no campsites open and a cold spell, daytime temperatures peaked at -10°C, and nights varied between -15°C to -21°C. We spent a month in these temperatures managing to ski occasionally, but it was very, very difficult and definitely not to be recommended. We skied the Spanish Pyrenees in March; it was warm, sunny and had good facilities. We had a very enjoyable experience and could have easily coped in any modern production motorhome- we are planning a ski trip with our Swift.

Self Build

Self building can be as rewarding as the use it's intended for, the opportunity to create a bespoke vehicle for your desires or needs. This will be difficult and extremely time consuming. Self build kits and specialist companies can assist leaving you to do the bits you are interested in. Self builds will not achieve the same resale price as a recognised brand.

'Self-build...bespoke'

Further Information

The Build Your Own Motorcaravan by John Wickersham, a Haynes publication 2006 is essential. Available from Haynes Tel: 01963 442030, bookshops and presumably libraries in due course.

The web site www.worldofmotorhomes.com may be able to help source parts and check the small ads in motorhome magazines.

The Motorcaravaner Club produces a booklet entitled The Official Home Conversion Guide costing £8.25 and available only to members. www.motorcaravanners.org.uk

www.jollyinteresting.co.uk is a website documenting a self build story. Club Care, Tel: 01784 484648, can assist in gaining insurance cover for self builds.

Visit motorhome/caravan shows to meet sellers of parts and look at existing vehicles to formulate ideas. A list of caravan breakers is available from The Caravan Club.

The motorhome as a lifestyle

Full-timing

Some people opt to leave bricks and mortar behind, living solely in their motorhome.

Anyone considering living in a motorhome full time should think very, very carefully. We have met people that call themselves full-timers. Of those, two couples lived in their American motorhomes 365 days of the year. One couple, two years in, were still trying to find a permanent pitch somewhere. Other touring couples regularly return to their UK base or take long non-motorhome holidays. We have met several single gentlemen living, working and touring in both motorhomes and caravans within the UK. Most full timers have an income from pensions, savings, rent or work part of the year. Touring full time is mentally and physically demanding and Europe suddenly becomes very small. The perception of full timing is highly romanticised. In reality, most full timers have extended periods of campsite recuperation normally through the winter. Our recommendation for anyone considering long term motorhoming is that they keep a base that they return to regularly.

We also met a couple that alternate between their narrow boat and wintering in their motorhome, which seems a very agreeable option.

Everyone needs to organise their administration however they live.

Having always holidayed in Greece, a British couple were extremely lucky finding their ideal campsite. They flew home and packed up their aged American motorhome. On arrival they stayed for two months on a touring pitch before committing themselves permanently. They chose an American motorhome because of the storage and living space. They have lived at the campsite for several years and even have enough space to grow vegetables. They expect the motorhome will be towed away for scrap eventually.

Where to stay

Where you wish to stay will influence the type of leisure vehicle you can take. Campsites are suitable for most motorhomes and caravans but owners of large motorhomes will have to choose campsites carefully, ensuring suitable access and pitches. Those wishing to take advantage of camper-stops, for economy or location, require a motorhome as only Italian camper-stops allow caravans. In countries where free-parking is legal, this applies to both motorhomes and caravans. Safety is greatly improved when free-parking in a motorhome as you can leave at a moment's notice without exiting the vehicle. Petrol stations, restaurants and pubs are often willing to allow motorhomes to stop overnight when making a purchase.

Campsites

There are around 30,000 campsites in Europe in all sizes and quality, for every budget and requirement. Campsites are well signed. There are plenty of publications with detailed information and discount schemes are available.

Small camping sites

Virtually every European country has small sites, ranging from gardens to farms, many with limited facilities, but often in unique locations.

Camper-stops

There are over 6,000 designated areas for motorhomes in Europe, providing parking, dumping and overnight facilities. Supported by the local community these bring welcome tourists into major and undiscovered areas alike, from town squares to tiny hamlets, frequently in stunning locations. These are free or a nominal charge might be made but only available to self-sufficient motorhomes.

We left the UK inexperienced and unsure of the systems abroad. Once there we discovered the laid back nature of European motorhoming. Out of season, campsites are relaxed and unannounced booking-in is welcomed. Camper-stops work on a first come first served basis, none were busy out of season. We also regularly free-parked. It didn't take long for us to relax into the continental motorhome way.

Free-parking

Also known as 'wild / free camping'. Many countries allow stopping overnight by the side of the road, ideal for those passing through, and equally suitable for those who enjoy remote locations. A privilege sometimes taken that truly identifies the freedom of motorhoming.

Types of Motorhome Travel

Everyone has his own idea of how he wishes to travel. Motorhomers are no exception.

Touring

The motorhome provides ultimate freedom moving on a whim, setting your own pace and itinerary. A motorhome is so convenient, that people touring move, on average, every two to three days. Setting and packing up takes minutes. Utilising the thousands of camper-stops across Europe not only allows ease of travel but also the discovery of otherwise unvisited places. People wishing to tour at a more leisurely pace, using campsites and moving every week or so, could easily tour with a caravan.

Solo destination

Normally based in one place, usually a campsite, for the entire duration. Many campsites focus on this type of user, providing a comfortable, affordable 'home from home' environment.

Single campsite stays allow enhanced enjoyment of the local and campsite community. All motorhomes are suitable for this type of holiday, although a caravan and car provide the best solution.

Escorted

There are various levels of escorted holidays, from booking ferries and campsites, to wintering in Spain, to adventure tours to China. Durations vary from a week to several months.

GB Privilege www.gbprivilege.com Tel: 01953 789661

TCH Holidays www.tchholidays.co.uk Tel: 01743 242354

The Caravan Club www.caravanclub.co.uk Tel: 01342 316101

The Camping and Caravan Club www.campingandcaravanning-club.co.uk Tel: 02476 422024

Perestroika Tours www.mir-tours.de Tel: Germany 06746 80280

Independent

The motorhome provides an unrivalled level of independence, unrestricted by tour operators, seasons or public transport, and is probably the best and cheapest way to discover Europe.

The motorhome reality

There are many different types of motorhome available. Despite the choice, you are unlikely to find one that meets all your criteria. Therefore, it is unlikely that the first motorhome you purchase will be exactly what you need. Hiring or borrowing a motorhome before you commit thousands of pounds will help you understand the compromises. Alternatively, keep a close eye on the second hand market. Find a good, clean motorhome at a sensible price even if it is not exactly what you're looking for. Ideally buy from a private seller to avoid the dealer's mark-up - remember they have to make a living but provide more consumer protection. Re-sell after six months when you have a better idea of what compromises you are prepared to make. Hopefully the motorhome will have cost no more than a two-week hire, especially if you have avoided the temptation to buy add-ons.

Size does matter; many campsites and smaller farm sites cannot cope with large motorhomes. Some camper-stops will be impossible to get to. Small can be equally stressful, so to illustrate this, here are a few real life examples we have encountered.

We met a family in the South of France touring Europe in an awesome 32 foot American motorhome, towing a Cinquecento. They were having a lovely time and found the motorhome very comfortable. Eight months into their tour they explained they couldn't get the motorhome on to most campsites due to narrow entrances, low trees and small pitches. When they did find a suitable campsite the only way they could discover the surrounding area was to fill the car, abandon the motorhome and set off. They had rented apartments and hotel rooms, effectively leaving the motorhome in storage to allow them to tour as they had intended.

Our 6.5m motorhome was very comfortable, although even this length prevented us driving down enticing tracks and lanes. Our present motorhome, a C class, just over five metres with a rear bed option is very versatile. We have travelled all over, Exmoor, Dartmoor and London and are confident enough to attempt even the most difficult looking tracks and lanes.

A Canadian couple we met a year into their tour, in a small VW camper, were managing to survive. They lacked storage, so had boxes filling all but the front seats. These had to be removed and placed under the awning every night. This rendered the motorhome unusable in the day, and was a real inconvenience to their trip. Some supervised camper-stops, were reluctant to let them stay, as they were not totally self-contained.

You can survive with any vehicle on even the lowest budget, but the dynamics of your trip will change accordingly.

We realise that some people simply don't want to tow, especially a large caravan. Having read this chapter if you think that a caravan would be more suitable for you, consider attending one of The Caravan Club's towing courses. These are reported to be very good and may help to make a decision. We make no secret of the fact that motorhomes are only better in certain situations and a good caravan/car can be purchased significantly cheaper.

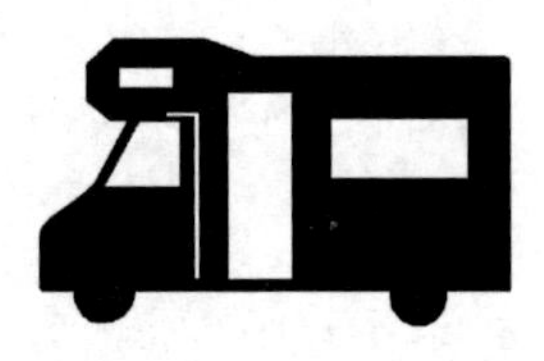

Chapter 2 - Buying your Motorhome

Dr Who's Tardis is the ultimate motorhome, a go anywhere vehicle with every creature comfort, but is presently unavailable! Manufacturers do offer over 1000 new models and there are over 50 years of earlier models. Whether you are one of the 8000 people a year who buy new or prefer second hand, the following information will ensure you ask the right questions.

Motorhome classes

Motorhomes are divided into three main categories, referred to as classes A, B and C.

Most motorhomes utilise an existing light commercial vehicle engine and chassis. Commonly used are Fiat-Citreön-Peugeot, Ducato-Relay-Boxer built in the same Seville factory. Others include Mercedes Sprinter, Iveco Daily, VW Transporter and Renault Master. Many motorhomes have been improved by grafting on an AL-KO galvanised chassis. This chassis has better suspension and floor platform giving enhanced road handling.

A-Class

Represents all motorhomes that are 'coach shaped' the smooth lined body added to a bare chassis cowl (engine, electrics, axles, suspension etc but not the cab). These may have a front drop down bed, but never a fixed over-cab bed like a C-Class.

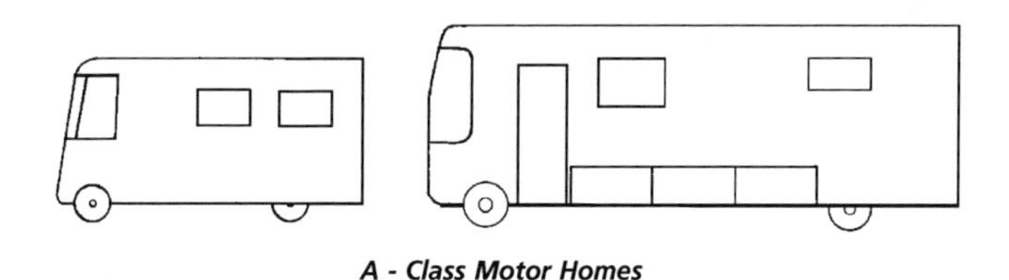

A - Class Motor Homes

B-Class

These are panel vans (transit vans) fitted out as motorhomes. These are also called day-vans and campervans. Not all have showers or separate toilet areas.

There are three types defined by headroom:

High top - An extra high solid fixed roof is added. Providing standing room or sleeping area over the living space.

Rising roof - This refers to motorhomes that are normal height in motion but once stationary the top can be elevated electronically or 'popped' up by hand to give extra height or a sleeping space.

Fixed roof - Utilises original van roof.

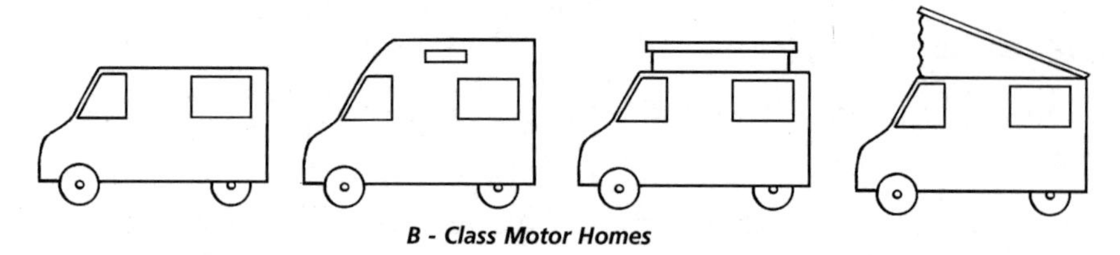

B - Class Motor Homes

C-Class

Refers to a chassis cab conversion with purpose built 'caravan' body attached.

Traditional style - These have a fixed sleeping area above the cab.

Low profile - The over cab fixed bed is removed, reducing the overall vehicle height.

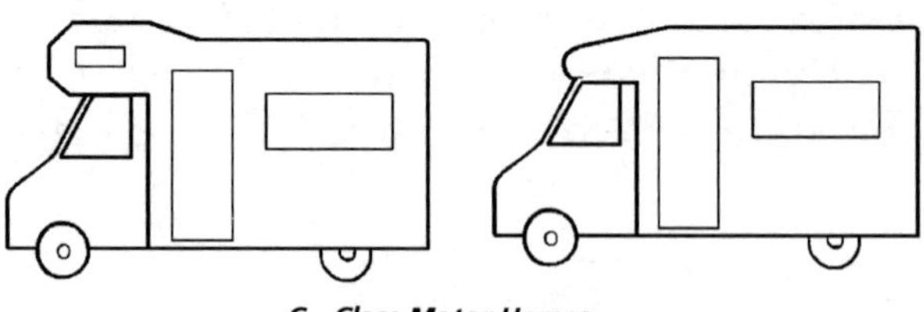

C - Class Motor Homes

Legal Considerations

The following factors should influence you when choosing a motorhome. There are legal implications especially concerning vehicle weights, driving licence restrictions and dimensions of motorhomes that prospective purchasers must understand. To be found, for example, to have overloaded your vehicle and thereby contributed to a fatal accident could well put you in severe difficulties. Throughout this book we stress the importance of not overloading because of the effect this can have upon handling, safety, stopping distances - you have been warned.

Maximum Technically Permissible Laden Mass (MTPLM)

Maximum Vehicle Weight, Gross Vehicle Weight (GVW), Maximum Technically Permissible Laden Mass (MTPLM) all refer to the legal maximum loaded weight including all occupants of a vehicle. Identified in the motorhome handbook and logbook as well as a plate fitted to the vehicle denoting all weight specifications. The plate is normally located in the engine housing and/or sometimes the foot wells. There are often the chassis manufacturer's and converter's plates on a vehicle; converters can have the vehicle weight re-assigned both up and down. The MTPLM should not be confused with the Gross Train Weight (GTW) a higher figure that specifies the maximum combined weight of the vehicle when towing a trailer. Driving licence restrictions apply: see below. Being caught driving a motorhome exceeding its MTPLM or GTW will at the very least result in a verbal warning. Recovery companies clearly state they may not recover vehicles they deem to be overloaded. Insurance companies may well not cover you if they discover the vehicle you were travelling in was contravening the law.

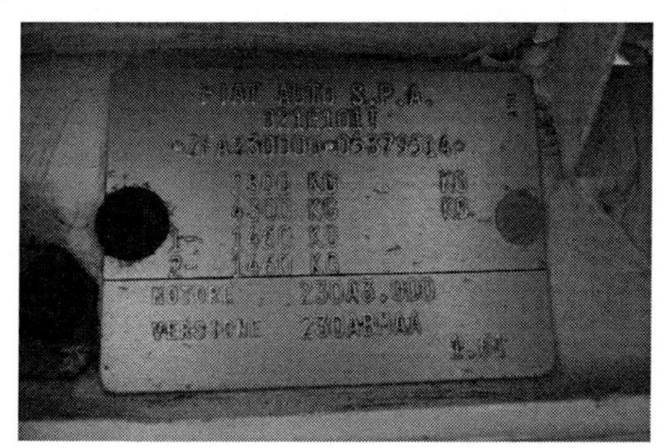

Payload

We cannot stress enough how important it is for you to understand payload, and we make reference to it throughout the book. Payload refers to the leftover weight between an empty motorhome (as calculated by manufacturers) and fully loaded to its specified MTPLM. We believe the payload should be sufficient in normal use to prevent you exceeding the MTPLM. Unfortunately this is not as straightforward as it seems as manufacturers include or exclude different items into the empty weight that is known as Mass In Running Order (MIRO).

Mass In Running Order (MIRO)

Refers to the entire manufactured weight of a vehicle and the equipment required to operate and in the case of motorhomes includes 'essential habitation equipment'.

Official MIRO and payload calculations - There are EU directives attached to 'The Road Vehicles (Construction and Use) Regulations'. These specify the calculations used to ascertain MIRO and payload. Currently each manufacturer interprets these differently. Harmonisation is due by July 2011 as all motorhomes will have to be 'type approved' the same as cars. Therefore motorhomes bought before then and subsequently second-hand may have different MIRO and payload calculations.

Manufacturers interpretation of MIRO - By referring to the Benchmark Motorhome chart it can be seen in the column entitled 'Not included in brochure MIRO' that Hymer include all 'essential habitation equipment' and allows for driver, electric cable and full, fuel/water tanks and gas bottles whereas Geist and Mclouis don't include anything not even the fuel. Therefore identical motorhomes on the same Fiat chassis with 100 litre water tanks can have a difference of 293 kg on their MIRO/payload weights. Many manufacturers can and will provide upgraded chassis, engines and base vehicles, as well as many optional extras. This information is available from dealers and websites, however the most reliable source is manufacturers' brochures. Magazine listings only show base models.

Many imported motorhomes are altered to suit British taste. These changes will alter vehicle weights but are not always clearly identified. To be absolutely sure a vehicle would have to be weighed. If you were just about to part with £25,000 plus, it would seem a reasonable request, as part of your test drive, to visit the local weighbridge.

Benchmark Motorhome chart - The authors believe that a motorhome is in 'running order' when; fuel tank is full, oils, coolant and jack are included, the freshwater tanks and gas bottles are also full, (after all you can't buy a 90% full gas bottle and why would you only fill the fuel tank to 90%), the driver's weight (EU regulation 75kg, 11st 12lb) and the electric hook-up cable are included into the MIRO before the payload is calculated. In addition we have added a passenger weighing 75kg into the calculations as nearly everybody we have met travel as a couple. This specification creates the 'Go Motorhoming adjusted MIRO' and it was used to calculate the 'Go Motorhoming payload'. To be included the motorhomes needed to have at least 500kg Go Motorhoming payload. As you can see from the chart this was no easy calculation. The key explains the elements used to adjust the brochure weights to the Go Motorhoming weight. In addition motorhomes had to meet the following criteria: no longer than six metres, contain at least a 100-litre fresh water tank and have at least one 11kg gas bottle. There are three sections to the chart, motorhomes up to 3500kg, motorhomes over 3500kg and near misses. Only A and C class motorhomes were evaluated because generally B class motorhomes have 500kg payload. However there are always exceptions to the rule and purchasers are advised the investigate payload toughly before buying a motorhome.

See The Benchmark Motorhome charts on the following pages, for motorhomes that meet the Go Motorhoming criteria.

Hidden Weight

Often overlooked is the 15/20 litres/kilograms of water in the boiler, pipe work and toilet flush. The authors could not find reference to whether or not leisure batteries were included. Only 75kg is calculated into the MIRO for the driver thus if the driver weighs 100kg, (15st 9lb) the actual payload is reduced by 25kg.

Chassis up-grades

It is possible on some models to have motorhome maximum weights re-assigned by DVLA. Often modifications to suspension and brakes are necessary. Contact TVAC (Drinkwater Engineering) for professional advice Tel: 01772 457116. When buying new it is sometimes possible to have a chassis upgrade and several motorhomes listed in the chart below are up-graded (UG) however they may need to be specially ordered. Up-grade information can be found in the technical specification section of sales brochures, but dealers may prefer to sell you something that's in stock.

Benchmark Motorhomes upto 3500kg

Manufacturer and brochure year	Model	Length (metres)	Fresh water (litres)	Gas bottles: number and size	MPTLM (Max weight kg)	Available Payload kg (as stated in brochure)	Not included in brochure MIRO	Weight in Kg to be deducted from brochures available payload	Go Motorhoming Payload (kg)
Auto Trail 2005	Tracker EK	5.72	81	7 & 13	3400	745	P, F=8, G=45, W=81, E	214	531
Auto Trail 2005	Tracker CK	5.72	81	7 & 13	3400	735	P, F=8, G=45, W=81, E	214	521
Auto Trail 2005	Tracker EKS	5.85	81	7 & 13	3400	715	P, F=8, G=45, W=81, E	214	501
Auto Trail 2006	Tracker EKS	5.85	81	7 & 13	3400	740	P, F=8, G=45, W=81, E	214	526
Burstner 2005	A-model 530	5.65	120	2x11	3500 UG	665	P, F=8, W90%=12, G=15	110	555
Burstner 2005	A-2-model 532-2	5.63	120	2x11	3500 UG	600	P, F=8, W90%=12, G=15	110	490
Burstner 2005	T-model T 585	5.99	100	2x11	3400/3500 UG	700/800	P, F=8, W90%=10, G=15	108	592/692
Burstner 2005/6	Elegance 590	5.9	140	2x11	3500	665	P, F=8, W90%=14, G=15	112	553
Burstner 2005/6	Elegance 591	5.9	140	2x11	3500	665	P, F=8, W90%=14, G=15	112	553
Burstner 2006	Marano T 580	5.99	120	2x11	3400/3500	770/880	P, F=8, W90%=12, G=15	110	660/760
Burstner 2006	Marano T 590	5.99	120	2x11	3400/3500	770/880	P, F=8, W90%=12, G=15	110	660/760
Burstner 2006	Marano T 595	5.99	120	2x11	3400/3500	730/830	P, F=8, W90%=12, G=15	110	620/720
Burstner 2006	Marano T 585	5.99	100	2x11	3400/3500	770/870	P, F=8, W90%=10, G=15	108	662/762
Burstner 2006	Lavanto A 530	5.4	120	2x11	3400/3500 FD15	640/740	P, F=8, W90%=12, G=15	110	530/630
Burstner 2006	Argos A532-2	5.63	120	2x11	3500	640	P, F=8 W90%=10 G=15	110	530
Chausson 2005/6	Welcome 55	5.99	128	2X11	3400	620	P, F=8, W=13, E, G=45	146	474
Dethleffs 2005/6	Globebus 1	5.79	115	2x11	3495	920/905	P, F=8	83	837/822
Dethleffs 2005/6	Globebus 2	5.79	115	2x11	3495	940/925	P, F=8	83	857/842
Dethleffs 2005/6	Globebus 3	5.79	95	2x11	3495	910/885	P, F=8	83	827/802
Dethleffs 2005	Advantage 5251	5.38	112	2x11	3495	827	P, F=8	83	744
Dethleffs 2005/6	Advantage 5831	6	112	2x11	3495	607/620	P, F=8	83	524/537
Dethleffs 2005/6	Advantage 5841	6.11	115	2x11	3495	755/765	P, F=8	83	672/682
Dethleffs 2005/6	Advantage 5841I	6.11	115	2x11	3495	1025/765	P, F=8	83	942/682

Dethleffs	2005	Premium T5846	6	110	2x11	3495	575	P, F=8	83	492
Dethleffs	2006	Fortero T 5915	5.96	110	2x11	3500	750	P, F=8	83	667
Dethleffs	2006	Fortero T 5975	5.96	110	2x11	3500	690	P, F=8	83	607
Geist	2005	Touring 55	5.99	100	2x11	3400	898	D, P, G=45 W=100, E, F=68	368	530
Home-car	2006	C25	5.59	95	7 & 11	3400	847/777/752	P, F=8, G=45, W=95, E, UG included	228	646/549/524
Hymer	2005	C class classic 514	5.61	100	2x11	3400/3500 UG	600/700	P, UG Included	75	525/625
Hymer	2005	c-class 494	5.19	90	2x11	3500 FD15 UG ccs	730	P, UG Included	75	655
Hymer	2005	c-class 544 K	5.61	120	2x11	3500 FD15 UG ccs	580	P, UG Included	75	505
Hymer	2005	c-class 524 GT	6.04	100	2x11	3500 FD18 UG	820/870	P, UG Included	75	745/795
Hymer	2006	c-class classic 544	5.98	120	2x11	3500 UG/ FD18 UG	625/595	P, UG Included	75	550/520
Hymer	2006	T-Classic 574	5.99	100	2x11	3400/3500 UG	650/750	P, UG Included	75	575/675
Hymer	2006	T-Classic 574	5.99	100	2x11	3500 FD18 UG	650	P, UG Included	75	575
Hymer	2005	B-class 504	5.99	70/120	2x11	3500	560	P	75	485
Hymer	2006	B-classic 504	5.99	120	2x11	3500 + FD18 UG	610/580	P, UG Included	75	535/505
Hymer	2006	Van 522	5.97	80	2x11	3500	920	P	75	845
Hymer	2006	Exsis SK	5.45	100	2x11	3500 FD15 UG	800	P, UG Included	75	725
Hymer	2006	Exsis SG	5.45	100	2x11	3500 FD15 UG	800	P, UG Included	75	725
Knaus	2006	ST 501L	5	115	2x11	3200	633	P, F=8	83	550
Knaus	2006	ST 501D	5.4	115	2x11	3200	583	P, F=8	83	500
Karman	2005	Colorado 550	5.685	100	2x11	3500	715	P, E G=15	95	620
Lunar	2005	Champ A520	5.59	95	7 & 11	3400 FD 2.3 UG	777	P, F =8, W=95, G=45, E	237	540
Mc louis	2005	Logan 253	5.99	100	2x11	3400 FD15 2.3 UG	1080	D, P, UG=120, W=100, G=45, E, F=68	488	592
Rapido	2005/6	7 Series 709F	5.56	120	7 &13	3400	585	P, F=8, G=2, W=12, E	102	483
TEC	2006	Rotec 582 Ti	5.989	120	2x11	3400/3500	680/780	P, F=8, G=15, W90%=12	110	570/670
TEC	2006	Rotec 560	5.731	120	2x11	3500	620	P, F=8, G=15, W90%=12	110	510
Weinsberg	2005	Orbiter 501	5.36	105	2x11	3500	722	P, F=8, G=45, E	133	589

(ccs) = camping car special
(D) = driver EU regulation 75kg
(E) = electric hook up cable estimate 5kg
(FD) = Fiat Ducato 15/18 referes to chassis 2.3/2.8 referes to engine
(F) = Fuel (diesel) @ .85kg per litre

(G) = filled bottle 6/7kg=15kg, 11kg=22.5kg, 13/15kg=30kg,
(P) = passenger @ 75kg each
(UG) upgrade engine/chassis
(W) = water 1kg per litre
90% of fuel, water or Gas can be included adjusted to 100%

Benchmark Motorhomes over 3500kg

Manufacturer and brochure year	Model	Length (metres)	Fresh water (litres)	Gas bottles: number and size	MPTLM (Max weight kg)	Available Payload kg (as stated in brochure)	Not included in brochure MIRO	Weight in Kg to be deducted from brochures available payload	Go Motorhoming Payload (kg)
Burstner 2005	T-model T585	5.99	100	2x11	3850	1070	P, F=8, W90%=10, G=15	108	962
Dethleffs 2005	Esprit A5810	6	150	2x11	3850	677	P, F 90%=8	83	594
Dethleffs 2005	Esprit I 5830	6.03	120	2x11	3850	557	P, F 90%=8	83	474
Geist 2005	Touring 55	5.99	100	2x11	3850 FD18/2.8 UG	1348	P, UG=75, D, G=45, W=100, E, F=80	464	884
Geist 2005	Phantom RG SWB	5.99	140	2x11	4600 MBS 416 UG	1464	P, UG=75, D, G=45, W=140, E, F=85	491	977
Hymer 2005/6	B-class 504	5.99	70/120	2x11	3900 FD18 AL-KO	920	P	75	845
Hymer 2006	B-classic 504	5.99	120	2x11	3850/3900	930/980	P, UG Included	75	855/905
Hymer 2006	B-classic 574	6.07	120	2x11	3850/3900	870/920	P, UG Included	75	805/830
Hymer 2005/6	B-class 564	6.07	70/120	2x11	3900 FD18 AL-KO	900	P	75	825
Hymer 2005/6	B-class 584	6.07	70/120	2x11	3900 FD18 AL-KO	850	P	75	775
Hymer 2005	c-class 544 GT	6.04	120	2x11	3850/3900	790/840	P, UG Included	75	715/765
Hymer 2006	c-class classic 544	5.98	120	2x11	3850/3900	945/995	P, UG Included	75	520/870/920
Hymer 2006	T-Classic 574	5.99	100	2x11	3850/3901	1000/1050	P, UG Included	75	925/975
Laika 2005	Ecovip H600	6	108	2x11	3850	808	P, F 90%=8 W90%=11 G=4	98	710
Niesmann B 05	Arto 59G	5.98	70/120	2x11	3850 FD18/2.8 UG	896	P, F 90%=8, G=2, W=57, UG 75	217	679
Pilote 2005	G600	6	130	2x13	3850	992	D, P, F 90%=8 G=23 W=23, E	209	783
Pilote 2005	G622	6.1	130	2x13	3850	725	P, F 90%=8, G=23, W=23, E	209	516
Rapido 2005	9 Series 924F	6	120	2x11	3850 FD18 AL-KO	790	F 90%=8 G=2 W=12, E, UG	137	653
TEC 2006	Rotec 5850 Ti	5.999	120	2x11	3850	920	P, F 90%=8, G=15, W90%=12	210	810

(ccs) = camping car special
(D) = driver EU regulation 75kg
(E) = electric hook up cable estimate 5kg
(FD) = Fiat Ducato 15/18 referes to chassis 2.3/2.8 referes to engine
(F) = Fuel (diesel) @ .85kg per litre

(G) = filled bottle 6/7kg=15kg, 11kg=22.5kg, 13/15kg=30kg,
(P) = passenger @ 75kg each
(UG) upgrade engine/chassis
(W) = water 1kg per litre
90% of fuel, water or Gas can be included adjusted to 100%

Motorhomes just outside benchmark specification

Manufacturer and brochure year	Model	Length (metres)	Fresh water (litres)	Gas bottles: number and size	MPTLM (Max weight kg)	Available Payload kg (as stated in brochure)	Not included in brochure MIRO	Weight in Kg to be deducted from brochures available payload	Go Motorhoming Payload (kg)
Ace 2005/6	Capri Low-Line	5.59	82	2x7	3400 UG	645	P, UG=70, F=8, G=2, W=8, E=5	158	487
Autocruise/ Pioneer 2005	Starlight/Cortes	5.59	72	2x7	3400	797	P, W=72, E, G=30	182	615
As above	Starmist/Marquette	6.115	72	2x7	3400	799	P, W=72, E, G=30	182	617
As above	Starburst/Renoir	6.154	77	2x7	3500	739	P, W=77, E, G=30	187	552
Compass/Elddis 06	Avant/Auto 100	5.356	70	2x7	3400	894	P, F=8, W=70, E, G=30	188	706
Compass/Elddis 06	Avant/Auto 120	5.356	82	2x7	3400	930	P, F=8, W=82, E, G=30	200	730
Compass/Elddis 06	Avant/Auto 130	5.829	70	2x7	3400	915	P, F=8, W=70, E, G=30	188	727
Compass/Elddis 06	Avant/Auto 140	5.829	82	2x7	3400	850	P, F=8 W=82, E, G=30	200	662
Compass/Elddis 06	Avant/Auto 150	5.829	82	2x7	3400	894	P, F=8, W=82, E, G=30	200	706
Compass/Elddis 06	Avant/Auto 160	6.1	82	2x7	3400	853	P, F=8, W=82, E, G=30	200	665
Knaus 2006	ST 605DKG	6.16	115	2x11	3500	628	P, F=8	83	545
Loudham Elddis 06	Sunstyle 100	5.49	70	2x7	3400	917	P, F=8 W=70 E G=30	188	729
Loudham Elddis 06	Sunstyle 120	5.49	76	2x7	3400	917	P, F=8 W=76 E G=30	193	724
Loudham Elddis 06	Sunstyle 130	5.91	70	2x7	3400	805	P, F=8 W=70 E G=30	188	617
Loudham Elddis 06	Sunstyle 140	5.91	76	2x7	3400	738	P, F=8 W=76 E G=30	193	545
Loudham Elddis 06	Sunstyle 150	5.91	76	2x7	3400	738	P, F=8 W=76 E G=30	193	545
Swift/Bessacarr 06	Sun 530LP / E410	5.59	82	2 x 7	3400 FD2.3 UG	715	P, UG=75, F=8, G=2, W=8 E=5	173	542

(ccs) = camping car special
(D) = driver EU regulation 75kg
(E) = electric hook up cable estimate 5kg
(FD) = Fiat Ducato 15/18 referes to chassis 2.3/2.8 referes to engine
(F) = Fuel (diesel) @ .85kg per litre

(G) = filled bottle 6/7kg=15kg, 11kg=22.5kg, 13/15kg=30kg,
(P) = passenger @ 75kg each
(UG) upgrade engine/chassis
(W) = water 1kg per litre
90% of fuel, water or Gas can be included adjusted to 100%

Second hand motorhomes

Previous owners will invariably have had additions or alterations. The only true way to know what payload is available is to include the above items and take the motorhome to a weighbridge. A reasonable weight of 575kg should be available for passengers, food, luggage and all other essential or desired items.

Axle weights

May total more than the maximum vehicle weight as this allows for load variation. Motorhomes with 60% overhang or longer increase the risk of exceeding rear axle weights. The most likely thing to cause an overloaded rear axle is 2/300kg of scooter and rack hanging off the back of a motorhome. Axles are always numbered from front to rear 1-2 and 3 when a tag axle is present.

Weighbridges

Are common but visit www.chrishodgetrucks.co.uk to find a local one. Weighbridges charge a small fee. If you do not require a print out this will probably be free, so take a pen and paper with you. Weigh the vehicle as a whole and then the front and rear axle as each of these has a maximum laden weight. In a paying situation only weigh the whole vehicle and one axle, the second axle weight is the remainder of total weight less the weighed axle.

Licence restrictions UK licence holders

If you passed your test before the 1 January 1997 you can drive a MTPLM of 7500kg and up to GTW of 8250kg if towing a trailer. Drivers reaching the age of 70 need to reapply for their driving licence and are restricted to 3500kg unless a medical is taken and submitted to the DVLA. If you have passed your test since 1 January 1997 you are limited to a maximum weight of 3500kg and limited to a maximum trailer weight of 750kg. To raise weight limit or trailer restriction on your licence, further driving tests need to be taken. Visit www.dvla.gov.uk, Tel: 0870 2400010 or pick up a form from the Post Office.

Motorhomes over 3500kg

As well as driving licence restrictions, motorhomes over 3500kg may also have to comply with other laws. It many countries speed restrictions apply. Some countries require additional road tolls to be paid while others treat any vehicle over 3500kg as commercial and expect them to comply with commercial regulations.

Size

In the United Kingdom the maximum permissible size of a motorhome is 12 metres (39′4") long and 2.55 metres (8′4") wide. Six metres is the benchmark between medium and large motorhomes. Campsites, road tolls, ferries, insurance and recovery prices are normally fixed up to six metres. A six metre motorhome will comfortably sleep 4/5 people, and can be driven almost everywhere. Six Metre rule - Six and below the benefits will show, anything more will be a chore. There are many points throughout this book, which support this statement, and if we were only giving one piece of advice it would be stay within six metres. ***See The Benchmark Motorhomes charts on pages 18 to 21 for a selection of motorhomes upto six meters***.

Wheelbase, overhang and clearance

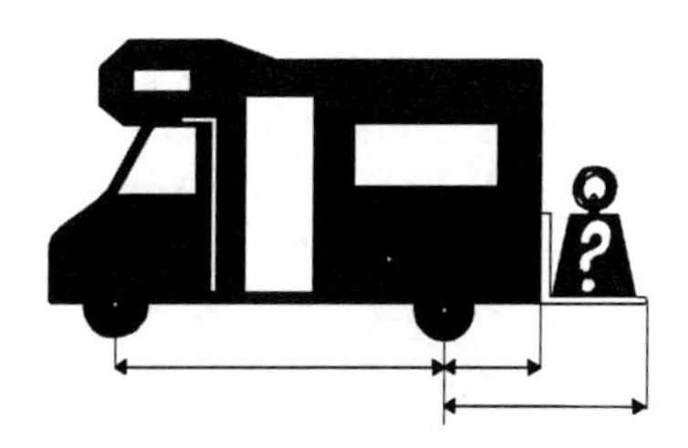

Wheelbase is the distance between the centre point of the front and rear wheels. Overhang; the distance from the centre point on the rear wheel to the rear of the motorhome ideally this should be less than 55 per cent of the wheelbase to allow for towbars or bike racks, however 60 per cent is the recognised maximum legal limit. We once measured a motorhome with a 71 per cent overhang. Large overhangs are easily scraped on uneven ground, steep ramps and can sag, especially if overloaded. When turning sharply be extremely careful not to tail swipe things, we speak from experience! In addition motorhomes low to the ground may struggle on uneven campsites and steep entrances, even if you don't venture off the beaten track.

Buying Considerations

Budget

Consider both the purchase price and running costs. As prices range from £1,000 to over £1,000,000 it is easy to become carried away, and you will probably find you need to spend more than you originally thought. Factor in insurance, servicing and recovery charges as well as fuel economy.

Availability of parts

Most internal living parts on European motorhomes are universal, therefore any camping and caravanning shop should be able to supply them. Parts and repairs on European base vehicles are not a problem. American and Japanese parts can be difficult and expensive to come by.

Fuel

As with the UK fuel prices vary dramatically across Europe and it's worth hunting around for the right deal. Diesel is considerably cheaper than unleaded fuel so it is worth choosing a diesel engine. Leaded petrol is not widely available on the continent, but the lead substitute added to unleaded fuel is. LPG is available on the continent but not widely in every country.

Condition

Check the overall condition including; chassis/underneath, engine, and mileage. Check the seals and trims on the outside for cracks, sun damage, knocks and scrapes. Inside check carpets, cupboards, handles and upholstery, be aware of any personalisation. Damp is a problem and must be checked for, but can normally be cured. It has a distinctive smell, mildew in cupboards is a sign but an inexpensive damp metre is worth having. Floors can de-laminate giving a bouncy feeling, again this can be cured. Wear and tear should be in line with the age of the motorhome. Ensure, by testing, that all gas/electricity parts are working. An older motorhome in excellent condition may be preferable to a younger one in poor condition.

Insulation

Those intending to visit conditions colder than the United Kingdom should look for motorhomes advertised as 'Winterised'. Anyone intending to ski should read the section on Cold Wintering in ***'When and where to go', chapter 7***.

Left or right hand drive

It is much easier to use a left hand drive in the UK than a right hand drive on the continent. Consider where you are going to drive most. People undertaking a grand tour, would be advantaged by having a left hand drive.

The living accommodation

Compromise is the only word that explains the situation. Thousands of layouts have been designed and continue to evolve, but there is no easy way to squeeze a kitchen, bathroom, dining room, lounge and bedrooms into a motorhome, so try not to be too ridged, as none of them will be perfect. If you are a couple this is the one time to be selfish. The occasional visiting friends or grandchildren should take the lowest priority on your layout choice. After all you can always put up a tent for them to sleep in. We believe that this is a reason why people buy motorhomes that turn out to be too big for them.

Bathroom - Not all motorhomes have a separate shower or a toilet, those who can rough it will survive without, but in reality this is inadequate. Those using free-parks and camper-stops must have their own facilities. A large bathroom is an unnecessary luxury as long as you can sit comfortably on the throne and has elbowroom in the shower. Our preference is a wet room designed without a material shower curtain. This design is the most space efficient and is kept clean; as every surface requires wiping down after showering, prompt wiping down also reduces condensation.

Bedroom/sleeping - Poor sleep can be a big problem, roughing it for a week can be fun, but after a month you may not be laughing. When we imported our Hymer 654 it had a home converted fixed rear bed with sprung slats and mattresses. This was as comfortable as our 4'6" luxurious bed in our American RV although a little smaller. We decided to return this conversion to the original lounge/bed option giving access to lockers, reducing weight and increasing versatility. With hindsight we would have slept better with Herr Heath Robinson's sleeping platform. The removed sprung slats were installed on the dropdown bed improving comfort and stopped the moisture problem where the mattress laid on the plywood base. This bed still proved uncomfortable after prolonged use simply because of the ageing foam mattress. The drop-down bed is a fantastic use of space, being easier to get in to than over-cab beds and is stowed away fully made up. The rear lounge bed was used mainly in hot conditions being closer to the floor and cooler air. This bed used the pedestal table as part of its construction; not only was this wobbly but the laminated surface caused the cushions to become wet. Cushions are attacked by mildew if not properly aired, this also occurs when seat cushions are directly against cold outside walls, properly 'winterised' motorhomes deal with this. Cab-over beds can be cramped, difficult to get into and very hot. They provide a space that we are happy to use.

'...This has the very latest over cab bed...'

Not only is it important to ensure that the bed is big enough but also the mattress or foam base is comfortable. Old foam deteriorates quickly and is relatively expensive to replace. Ensuring a good night's sleep well outweighs this cost. Bed slats prevent moisture building up, and sprung slats improve comfort. Ikea have a range of sprung slats. Also available are mattress liners that allow an air gap. Some beds are so close to the heater it could be dangerous.

Kitchen - Can be cramped so ensure there is enough space to prepare a meal, but as with bathrooms they only need to be just big enough. Markets and supermarkets are much cheaper than campsite shops, so storing food and keeping it cool is a necessity. A fridge and a freezer, no matter how small, are essential. Three rings are adequate to cook most meals, a grill is an added bonus. Ovens are not standard in most European motorhomes but are popular with the British and Americans. Although sometimes nice to have, ovens are far from essential and in every caravan/motorhome we have bought they appear to have been unused. Our personal view on ovens is that the loss of storage, additional weight and noise whilst travelling is not worth the occasional roast dinner. There are plenty of worktop electric ovens that can be purchased if desired and an electric oven is recommended for long term campsite stays.

Socialising/lounging- On cold, wet or mosquito plagued evenings you may be lounging or entertaining inside your motorhome. The traditional dinette set up can prove small and uncomfortable for long periods. L-shaped seating areas (still around a removable table) provide a more comfortable and sociable solution. Many motorhomes do not take advantage of dual function. The driver and passenger chairs should swivel to become armchairs (captain's chairs) but these are often said to be too high when driving because of the swivel mechanism. The sofa and dining area should become a bed without the use of the table, which should be able to free stand for outside use. Other design considerations include, correct location of TV, lights and plug sockets. Our Swift only has a woefully inadequate single 230v plug socket over the draining board. Seat cushions as with beds the foam condition and thickness is important and sprung seat cushions prove more comfortable both day and night.

Storage space - Consider where you are going to store everything. Are there enough lockers, can you get to the lockers from both inside and outside? Is the wardrobe efficient space? Some motorhomes have garages (large lockers at the rear) designed for bicycles, motorbikes or micro cars and some are converted to hold animals, domestic not farm yard variety. Garages are not essential and are easy to overload but bikes on racks get filthy in wet or dusty driving conditions no matter how well covered.

Extras/add-ons

These are items above the basic specification. These don't necessarily add any value but may be nice to have and indeed be on your own "must have" list. Try not to be swayed by these and remember they can add considerable weight and apart from proper alarms, solar panels and awnings are relatively cheap to add. See ***'Preparing Your Motorhome', Chapter 4.***

Disabled motorhomers

In 2006 SeA produced their first C class motorhome CPT. It has been designed for a wheelchair user and carer. Benimar produce the Euroable motorhome for disabled users. Several converters carry out alterations to new and second hand vehicles and are regularly seen at motorhome shows. Nirvana Motorhomes has a "try-before you-buy" scheme for disabled motorhomers www.nirvanarv.com Tel: 0800 3281475. Murvi, a multi award winning company Tel: 01752 892200 www.murvi.co.uk, builds panel van conversions to client specifications, with around 12 per cent of these having disabled features. We would seriously consider one if we wanted a B-class. www.roywoodtransits.co.uk Tel: Tel: 0118 9790202 have disabled solutions. See also Queen Elizabeth's foundation, www.qefd.org Tel: 01372841100. Forum for Mobility Centres help line Tel: 08700 434700. Disabled Caravan and Campers Group Tel: 01275 839961, and there is a mobility directory in the classified section of Practical Motorhome magazine.

Where to buy

Visiting dealers is a good starting point, you will be able to see many different motorhomes in one go, although often only one manufacturer's range. Motorhome shows attract several dealers who will be showing the majority of brands both new and second hand. These shows are advertised in all the magazines and listed on www.ukmotorhomes.net and held all over the country. Special ticket offers are normally available through the camping/caravan clubs as well as motorhome clubs. Dealers should have a wealth of information, so ask plenty of questions and try to imagine how you will live in the motorhome. Sit in the living space, pretend to cook a meal or have a shower, and make the bed up. Hiring prior to buying new is extremely sensible especially for those with no motorhoming or caravanning experience. Some dealers/hire companies offer the opportunity to have the hire fee refunded if you then buy a motorhome from them within a time limit. If a warranty is important to you then buying from a dealer (new or second hand) is your best option. You will pay more than from a private seller and could loose out when you sell. Warranties can be bought privately for motorhomes up to a specified age.

After identifying a particular type, make and model, look at adverts on Auto Trader www.autotrader.co.uk and www.mobile.de, the German version of Auto Trader, which will give you an idea of the prices abroad if you decide to buy an import. Visit www.motorcaravanning.co.uk or www.ukmotorhomes.net, websites that have classified sections. The 'free ads' papers are a good source of cheaper motorhomes. Private sales in the motorhoming magazines are often priced much higher than they actually sell for. Response to adverts can be low, so you should be able to negotiate. Having looked at all the options and you decide to buy new, use the listings in the back of the motorhome magazines to phone all the relevant dealers and see what you can negotiate over the phone. There is no reason why you should not buy a long way from home as many dealers have overnight facilities to use whilst motorhomes are in for servicing. If you have niggling problems these will be more of an issue. The September shows see dealers selling off the current year's stock in preparation for the new models. Those looking for a small motorhome or bargain should consider visiting Market Street in North London. Many motorhomes are brought and sold there primarily by Australian, New Zealand and South Africans who use them for european tours. The closer to flights home the cheaper the price gets. In recent years Ebay has also had its fair share of motorhome sales.

The Buyers Check List

Questions to ask either over the phone or to check when visiting seller.

- Describe the lay out of the motorhome starting from the cab: are the cab seats captain's chairs and do they swivel? Is there a separate bathroom with toilet and shower? Where are the beds and what size are they? Is the floor carpeted and is it removable?
- How long have you owned it and why are you selling?
- What is the MTPLM and payload? Does the MIRO weight include full fuel tank, driver, full water tank and full gas bottles? (If the seller is unsure or blasé then the likelihood is they have been using it overloaded, or in the case of a new motorhome has inadequate payload).
- Is there any damage to the vehicle, has it been accident repaired? Is there sun damage?
- What is the interior condition, where are the marks, scuffs or wear, how much wear is there on the cushions, is the foam starting to show signs of age? How clean/worn are the carpets?
- How often and where did you use the motorhome? How many miles has it done, how many have you done, and how many in the last year?
- What is the overall size of the motorhome? (will it fit on your drive).
- Is there any, or has there been any, damp?
- Is it diesel or petrol? Is the engine powerful enough? How many miles to the gallon? Does it use any oil?

- Has it had any DIY alterations or paint jobs?
- Is there anything that doesn't work properly or is broken?
- What kind of heating system does it have?
- Does the fridge have a freezer compartment?
- What hot water system is there, does it run on gas, electric or both?
- How accessible is the engine and what is it based on? Will the parts be available?
- What security features does it have, locks and alarms?
- Are there blinds and fly screens on the windows and top vents?
- How large is the water tank, where is it located and is any filter system fitted?
- Is there enough or too much storage? Are there any external lockers?
- What repairs have been done; new exhaust, how old are the tyres? Tyres over five years old will probably need replacing irrespective of tread depth.
- How does the toilet system work and how much capacity do the toilet and waste tanks have?
- What capacity is the leisure battery in amp hours and how old and how easy is it to access? Are there any 12v sockets? Does the motorhome have electric hook up and cable and where are the sockets located and how many are there?
- What add-ons or extras come with it?
- How many and what size gas bottles does it take, are the gas bottles included?
- What service history does it have, does it have its original documents i.e. manuals, when did it have its last MOT, engine chassis and habitation service and by whom?

- Can you arrange for us to take the motorhome to a weigh-bridge during our test-drive?
- What warranty is included and what are the conditions i.e. return to base or Europe wide?
- How did you come to the advertised price and have you since reduced it? (only ask this question toward the end as it may affect the way a seller answers further questions).

It is the authors' experience when buying privately, that an owner who answers these questions confidently and willingly over the phone is selling a genuine motorhome in the condition described. The main problem will be convincing them that they should sell you the motorhome at the price you think its worth. When the alleged owner answers questions poorly, is evasive or repeatedly says "it's a good runner - a really nice camper" then the chances are you will see a different motorhome than the one you had in mind. So expect to be on the phone for 20 minutes and unless you are completely sure, don't bother to drive a long distance to see a private sale motorhome. Equally don't fall in love with it before you've seen it. One final point people prefer you to be honest, so whether on the phone or at a viewing if it's not right for you stop there and tell them so and why. "I will think about it" at the end of a long period of someone's personal time is frustrating.

Professional opinion

If you are not sufficiently competent, seriously consider getting a professional inspection. Motoring recovery organisations will carry out mechanical inspections, but will not be able to comment on the 'caravan' side of things. The best option if possible would be to take it to a motorhome service centre.

Selling

When selling your motorhome it is important not to overprice it. This only wastes your time and money. Expect your motorhome to depreciate, how much depends on age and condition. Dealers will often negotiate a price over the phone, but they will err on the side of caution. Use this price to assess a sensible price, comparing private and dealer adverts for similar motorhomes. Remember dealers mark up between £2000 and £6000; they also add at least

£1000 for negotiation. Motorhomes advertised in the magazines that are priced on the cheap side of realistic sell very quickly. Part exchanging is unlikely to be the most economical but offers a simple solution. The MMM magazine publishes a six part second hand price guide, but only shows dealer forecourt prices of available models. Additions don't necessarily add value but may make your motorhome more sellable. Remember that any DIY, repairs or 'interior design' will detract from the sale price if it doesn't appear to be a professional job.

Clean the motorhome really thoroughly (dealers do) and remove anything that is not included in the sale. Provide as much information about the vehicle as possible, have it MOT'd and if you're selling from your drive make it presentable. Park so the vehicle can be inspected on all sides. Finally don't warm it up before a viewing, buyers will be suspicious about its starting ability. Batteries are cheap, replace if necessary.

Most prospective buyers have an idea of what they want. It is worth asking them on the phone which models they like and how they intend to use one. We always do this and apart from people who live locally, discourage others if we know it is unsuitable for them. We have had good response from websites, some success from Auto Trader, although the endless sales calls from people wanting to send free information or having buyers looking for a 'Winnibago campervan' are enough to put us off. The Motor Caravan magazine advertises private sales free, use this and free websites first. Don't be discouraged by callers who arrange to view only to cancel on the day. Remember you also had no idea what you wanted at some stage.

Test driving

Test-drives are essential but only to people who are seriously interested. It is unlikely that a prospective buyer has sufficient insurance cover. If you do have fully comprehensive 'any vehicle' insurance, take proof with you. Personally if a buyer with relevant insurance really wants to drive I would take them to a deserted car park. Even from the passenger's seat it is possible to assess the vehicle condition, and the way it has been driven. Look for clutch travel and whether the driver uses the pedal as a footrest. Listen and watch for smooth gear changes, including reverse. Take the vehicle on a dual carriageway and up a steep hill and on twisty roads, all give an overall impression. Take the opportunity to visit a weighbridge and find out exactly what payload is available. Finally security; people do steal vehicles whilst on test-drives so stay with them at all times or when they have access to the keys.

Further Information

Auto Trader has detailed information with tips for buyers and sellers at the start of its magazines and on line at www.autotrader.co.uk. This information details everything from how to write your advert, what questions to ask and security checking the vehicle for damage, theft, or outstanding finance, something we definitely recommend doing.

Importing from Europe and beyond

It is relatively easy to import vehicles from the EU, although the DVLA should be contacted before undertaking any importation to check any changes to forms or procedures. Contact the DVLA on www.dvla.gov.uk or Tel: 0870 2400010 and request either V55/5 for used vehicles or a V55/4 for new, these forms are an 'application for a first licence for a used/new motor vehicle and declaration for registration'. Also request forms INF106 'Import (Information) Pack' and supporting information. New vehicles can only be registered brand new: if they have reasonable delivery mileage, have not been previously permanently registered, are a current model or ceased production within the last two years.

The urgent task is registering quickly within 14 days of purchase. Once in the UK a used vehicle, older than three years from first registration in the country of origin, needs to pass an MOT. Some alterations may be needed; headlights corrected/changed, fog light on the offside and the speedometer having mph graduations that are visible at night. A Whole Type Vehicle Approval is required for cars that are younger than 10 years old, this is not needed nor a SVA test as motorhomes are exempt. Your local DVLA office, however, may request an inspection of the vehicle.

The following information needs to be sent or taken to your local DVLA office:

- V55/5 or V55/4
- The MOT certificate,
- The original copy of UK vehicle insurance certificate,
- A utility or bank statement,
- Personal identification: passport or driving licence paper copy,
- The export papers including the equivalents of the UK log book that needs to show the date of first registration.

Vehicles over 6 months old which have travelled more than 6000 kms (3,750 miles) will not be subject to VAT and will be self declared on form VAT 414.Vehicles imported from outside the EU need form C&E 386; these are required by HM Revenue and Customs for a vehicle of any age personally imported, to assess any VAT due.

- All imported vehicles need to be stored off the public highway until registration is completed.
- Vehicles can be driven to and from MOT stations/garages for purposes of test and repair.
- Your normal insurer may not be able to insure the unregistered vehicle. Insurance is a legal requirement if used on the road and suitable third party insurance brokers can found by contacting British Insurance Brokers Association on Tel: 0207 623 9043 or emailing enquiries@biba.org.uk

European motorhomes

Ranges of motorhome are available on the continent that have rarely been seen in the UK. There are many more types and styles available in Germany, France, the Netherlands and Italy where an import can be found. Buying in continental Europe can also save considerable money but this is dependent on exchange rates. The only problem with buying an unknown brand or model is that it may prove harder to sell.

Some European dealers advertise in motorhome magazines, visit www.mobile.de to find German dealers. Not all dealers speak English but many advertise that they do. Ask if they offer an export service, when the paper work and number plates for export should be provided. This is inexpensive and reduces complications. German dealers do not accept cheques, bank drafts or debit cards and are reluctant to accept credit cards due to high charges. Therefore only two options remain, cash or a telegraphic transfer from your bank account. Speak to your branch to discuss how to do this. Ideally do not pay for the motorhome until you have inspected it. German export number plates are issued with 14 days use and third party insurance. It would be wise to stop a night or so to check everything over just in case there are any problems. Articles on importing are available on www.motorhomefacts.com

American motorhomes

These come in all shapes and sizes, are usually large and luxurious with mod cons to match. Importing an American motorhome can prove very cost-effective, with many dealers on the internet. Importing is not without its pitfalls as some American motorhomes are illegal in the United Kingdom due to their size. They must not be wider than 8′4" (2.55 metres) or longer than 39′4" (12 metres). Don't forget shipping will have to be arranged. Contact the American motorhome clubs as some members have imported and have a wealth of knowledge and experience.

Japanese/ New Zealand Imports

These tend to be smaller vehicles without the same running expense and size issues of American models. Do research the availability of parts before purchasing. There are several companies now importing from these countries.

Having searched for months we decided to buy a left hand drive Hymer B654. We viewed one at a dealer in the Midlands that turned out to be the same age, condition and mileage as the one we imported. The best price we negotiated after an hour in the dealer's office, getting a £2000 discount, was £21,000. We soon found an identical B654 in Bremen, Germany. After a few phone calls and emails with photos, we arranged to buy. We flew out carrying a small handful of €500 notes, were met at the airport and did the deal. There was definitely an element of risk but we paid (including all costs, travel, UK MOT and registration) just under £15,000, including an engine and running gear warranty that covered us for the whole of Europe.

Chapter 3 - Utilities (consumable)

It is difficult to work out how long the utilities of 12v electricity, gas and water will last and how to use them efficiently. Having recorded our utility use and that of others this section gives real examples to unravel the realities.

Electricity

Although water is fundamental to life there is more written about electricity or at least the lack of it than all the other utilities put together. There are countless gadgets that can be purchased that use, modify or generate electricity. Before you rush to the shops it's worth considering the information below. It is after all, the reality.

Electricity both 12v and 230v have inherent dangers, 230 volt has sufficient energy to cause a fatality and a 12v short circuit could start a fire. We do not condone unsafe practices nor is the following an installation manual we merely make the following general comments. When considering carrying out any maintenance, repair or installations seek professional advice. All leisure vehicles as part of their annual service should have the electrical systems inspected by a qualified electrician. Second hand vehicles without supporting documentation should also be checked; if in doubt seek professional advice.

Using 12 volt electricity

No matter what you do, this is always a limited supply. Available power is determined by the capacity of batteries, their condition and charge state. Assuming the motorhome has a leisure battery in addition to an engine battery, (all but the oldest and small day vans do) flattening the leisure battery is barely an issue. Even following a long day's driving, after watching about 3 hours satellite television the lights would dim and the TV would turn off signalling bedtime. Manufacturers, with the exception of Elecsol warn against fully discharging a battery. We had a standard lead acid 110 Amp hour leisure battery, which gave very good readings on a hydrometer after a year and a half of constant use. The alternator and charger were also standard units.

Battery selection

To ensure you have enough power for your 12 volt system the correct battery needs to be selected. Batteries are rated in Ampere Hours (Ah) therefore you need to calculate the Ah's you think you will use daily. To do this work out the amperage of all the items you will use (or would like to use) and for how long. Amps can be calculated by dividing watts by volts, therefore a 1000w fan heater runs at 4.35A, 1000w / 230v = 4.35A. If the fan heater could run on 12v then it would use 83.33A in an hour clearly a problem when only one 75Ah battery is installed. In reality most C class motorhomes house the leisure battery under a cab seat, so if you divide the figure you had previously calculated by 10 that'll be the size of battery you will be able to have. The largest capacity battery fitting in this space is more than sufficient for 5-7 days, without TV. A second battery can be located under the other seat and run in parallel but must be properly installed, secured and vented. The basic rules are the batteries need to be the same age, type and capacity. They are connected together positive-to-positive, negative-to-negative. This type of connection makes the two batteries become one, but the charger will stop once one of the batteries is fully charged. Therefore any discrepancy in capacity or condition of the batteries will result in a lower than expected quantity of Ah's available.

Battery chargers are normally specific to type, either lead acid or gel, this is due to different charging requirements. The charge rate in Ah should be 10 to a maximum of 20 per cent of the batteries Ah's capacities, i.e. 7.5 amps for a 75Ah battery and 10 amps for a 100 Ah battery. Gel batteries must only be charged to a maximum 14.4v to prevent gassing.

According to manufacturers the optimum-operating temperature for a battery is around 27°C (80°F). Available battery power reduces approximately one per cent (1A) per 1°C fall in temperature. Therefore at freezing point a batteries capacity is reduced by approximately 27 per cent. Batteries may be rated as being 110Ah but only discharges to between 50- 80 per cent therefore in optimum conditions 88Ah is available but may be as low as 55Ah.

Our recommendation is that standard lead acid leisure batteries are suitable for most motorhome and caravan users. They are far cheaper than AGM or gel alternatives and as long as they are looked after will last several years. Do insure they are topped up regularly with demineralised water and charged occasionally during lay up periods. Nearly all lead acid batteries have some carbon fibres in their composition. Starter and leisure batteries are basically the same, but are modified to suit the demands of the different applications. Having said that some manufacturers advertise that their batteries do both jobs. People who will always 'hook up' or will only stop a night or two need only buy a small capacity leisure battery.

Whilst parked by a Bulgarian ski lift, our 110Ah battery powered the motorhome's systems. We managed two days and nights. Daytime temperatures peaked at -15°C and dropped to an unbelievable -21°C both nights. We had the blown air heating on constantly and lights on from 5 pm - 10.30 pm, and the battery had sufficient power for another night. Unfortunately the gas regulator froze on the second night, and we were woken by the cold at 3 a.m. The driver was promptly promoted to chief engineer and various efforts to alleviate the problem failed. Thankfully we had saved the long hose from a gas BBQ that we had discarded months before, and used the hose to bring the gas bottle with regulator attached inside. We don't recommend this practice but in the situation the action was appropriate. We decided to move on as soon as the car park opened and returned the gas bottle to its proper place.

See Add-ons and extras Chapter 4 covering both generating equipment and using 12 volt.

Inverters (12v to 230v)

It is possible to use appliances designed for mains electricity in the motorhome, even when not plugged in. An inverter converts 12v Dc into 230v Ac and does this at about 80 to 90 per cent efficiency, Moore power say their inverters are 94 per cent efficient Tel: 01273 615384 www.moore-power.co.uk. To ensure best efficiency and reduce the chance of damaging equipment, work out what you wish to run and speak to a specialist before choosing appliances. There are many 12v appliances available ranging from kettles and hairdryers to televisions and microwave ovens, so consider these before opting for an inverter. In reality many motorhomers use inverters simply for their satellite system or laptop. Using appliances of higher amperage than the 12v Dc system can cope with, especially an inverter may result in a fuse being blown or cables and plug sockets overheating. This in turn could damage the appliance or start a fire. Always check the appliances amperage before using and ensure that fuses and wiring are appropriate. It is probably best to have a short dedicated connection between the leisure battery and inverter. Sterling Power Products Ltd specialises in inverters, www.sterling-power.com Tel: 01905 453999.

Regulators (12v to 12v)

Equipment that has external transformers such as laptops can use regulated 12v rather than use the original 230v - 12v transformer. Action Replay sells one such device that is capable of running just about any 12v device up to 60w. Their website has pictures of about 20 connector plugs that fit most equipment. This regulator is also about 80 per cent efficient. Contact Action Replay on Tel: 05511 436245 normal rate or www.action-replay.co.uk

12 volt Electricity consumption - the reality

Generally available guidance suggests a 75Ah battery used only for the water pump and lights when necessary, will have sufficient power for a pitched week in the summer. With a second/larger battery or a solar panel it will possibly last for two weeks. The longest we have solely relied on a 110Ah battery between charges is two summer weeks. The same amount of power is used in one night watching satellite TV powered by an inverter. Tourers moving every few days should find they charge their batteries sufficiently without the need of electric 'hook-up'. We monitored 298 continuous days away, during which we hooked up for 86 nights. We would have hooked up for only 11 nights had electricity not been included in campsite fees. We were not alone in this usage as most tourers we've met followed the same practices.

Compressor fridges only run on 12v, and apart from on expedition vehicles, are unnecessary. Although compressor fridges can operate in hotter temperatures we successfully used our standard three-way absorption fridge on gas in 37°c.

The RoadPro website www.roadpro.co.uk or catalogue is essential for all motorhomers. It provides detailed technical information in plain English covering electrical systems and appliances within their products range including inverters, solar panels, advanced chargers, and compressor fridges. The extracts written by Charles Watts of Stirling Power provide an in-depth discussion about batteries and a compelling argument for advanced chargers. RoadPro is a motorhome-owning company whose owner free-parks and understands the issues and constraints.

A small range of leisure batteries

Manufacturer	Model	AH	Weight KG	Dimensions L x W x H (mm)
Energy	SFL 2	110	28	330 x 175 x 220
Energy	AGM 85	85	23	260 x 169 x 213
Energy	AGM 100	100	27	260 x 169 x 213
Energy	AGM 110	110	33	331 x 174 x 220
Energy	GEL 110	100	33	330 x 174 x 220
Powermax	85/LEISURE	85	18.5	245 x 173 x 205
Powermax	110/LEISURE	110	27	345 x 173 x 230
Hi fase	GP70	70	17.5	255 x 173 x 208
Hi fase	GP85	85	18.5	225 x 173 x 208
Hi fase	GP110	110	28.5	345 x 175 x 226
Varta	95752	90	23.8	353 x 175 x 190
Varta	95851	100	24.6	305 x 175 x 220
Elecsol	Elecsol 100	100	19.6	278 x 175 x 190
Elecsol	Elecsol 110	110	25.2	353 x 175 x 190
Elecsol	Elecsol 125	125	28.5	344 x 172 x 235

Specifications courtesy of Barden UK Ltd, Dynamic Battery Services Ltd and Elecsol Europe

AGM – absorbed glass mat, these batteries perform in a similar way to gel batteries being sealed and leak proof.

Dynamic Battery Services Ltd, Tel:01695 557575 Hi fase

www.barden-uk.com Tel:01489 570770 energy, Powermax and Varta

www.elecsol.com Tel:0800 163298 Elecsol

The available space under the driver's seat of our 1997 Fiat motorhome is approximately 360mm long x 200mm wide x 230mm high. Height is the greatest concern, as precautionary measures need to ensure the terminals do not arc or touch the metal frame of the seat. Proprietary snap on terminal connecters with colour coded plastic covers are available from most camping shops. A second tip given to us by Dynamic Battery Services is to cover the battery with a rubber floor mat used in car foot wells.

Electric hook up

A 25 metre hook-up cable is necessary as electricity points can be sited some way from the pitch, or level area. Be aware that not all campsites or camper-stops use the blue 'leisure' socket, many still use the domestic plug of the country. The blue socket in industrial use identifies the source to be 230v. A mini extension with a leisure plug one end and a continental two-pin plug is a necessity. These are widely available but ensure there are earthing straps on the outer casing and a hole in the face of the plug for use in France. Leisure plugs are designed to be used outside, by attaching a domestic plug it is no longer rain proof. A commonly seen water proofing system is covering the plugs with a watertight bag taped with heavy duty (gaffer) tape.

At camper-stops there may be one or two plug sockets available, if electricity is free or included in the price then 'double plugging' may occur. Although on a first come, first served basis electricity could end up being shared by up to three motorhomes. In this situation it is vital to be aware of your safety. If you are confident that the situation is safe be aware that very low electricity consumption is necessary. Putting both the kettle and fan heater on simultaneously may trip the supply and may not be able to be reinstated.

Many hook ups abroad are only 3A, not the 16A we are used to in the UK. If 6A – 9A, or higher is available it will be priced accordingly and can be significantly more expensive. When purchasing electrical items bear this in mind as you may trip the electrics, not just your pitch but also the whole row! Most British sites now install 16A as standard.

Calculating amps

To know if you have enough amps to run appliances follow the equation:

$$\frac{\text{Number of watts}}{\text{Number of volts}} = \text{number of amps}$$

Our television operates on both 12v and mains electricity. When the TV is operated from the mains, the amps being used will be 35 watts/230 volts=0.15 Amps. The same TV on 12v is 60 watts/12 volts= 5 Amps. Appliances usually display a label denoting electrical specifications.

By calculating your electricity consumption you can calculate if you require 3, 6, or 9A electric hook up.

Reversed polarity

There is a problem called 'reversed polarity' on some continental sites. Apart from France who have a three pin system the rest of the European countries that we visit have plugs with two pins and two earth bonding straps (metal strips) on the outer casing of the plug. This means the plug can go in either way round. Therefore it is irrelevant which way live and neutral are wired. Plug in appliances sold on the continent are designed to cope with live/neutral either way round. For safety it is recommended that UK users check each time they hook up abroad. Firstly turn off all appliances including fridge and battery charger. Turn main trip switch to OFF position and plug in hook-up cable. A simple detector, available in camping and electrical wholesale shops, is plugged into one of the motorhomes domestic three pin sockets. Switch trip ON and the lights on the detector indicate the presence of earth and the direction of polarity. If polarity is reversed when using a two pin domestic plug simply pull out and turn over. When using French or blue leisure plug there are two options. First disconnect and re-wire the plugs live and neutral or have a second short extension with live and neutral reversed. A polarity changeover switch is available from Riversway Leisure www.riverswayleisure.co.uk Tel: 01772 729999 that simply switches the incoming current.

The Caravan Club Europe book details this as does the *Motorcaravan Manual* and *Caravan Manual* by John Wickersham with several useful pictures.

Getting the most from mains electricity

Whenever you pay for mains electricity it is worth getting value for money. Recommended are a low watt electric kettle and cooking ring. Both are available from electrical stores and Argos. Don't believe that all electrical goods are cheaper on the continent as this is not always the case.

A dual function electric fan heater/cooling fan should be taken. These often have step heat/power levels, and will work on a 3amp supply. These are especially good if they are thermostatic switching on and off according to temperature. Other than these three items everything else is a luxury you could take if you have weight and space available.

Water heaters that have a mains element draw about 2.75 amps. If tripping is likely simply managing electrical draw by heating water then turn off. Heated water will stay warm for several hours. Retro fitting a water heating element is unlikely to be cost effective especially if a refillable gas bottle is used.

Free Electricity - In France many camper-stops have access to free power. Look for free camper-stops which have 230v mentioned in *Le Guide National des Aires de Services camping-cars* available from hypermarkets in France. Very useful in winter when heat is essential and camper-stops are quiet. Many other countries' camper-stops have electricity available at minimal cost.

Solar panels

If you intend to free-park long term, you may consider a solar panel though this is realistically only likely in Morocco. Given the initial expense and that they are most needed in the winter when the days are short there is mixed response in the motorhoming community to their value. Motorhomers we have spoken to say their solar panels extend battery life to two weeks instead of one, as opposed to being able to maintain the battery charge. They certainly will not provide enough power to watch TV every night.

If you are considering a solar panel there are various factors; first the least effective solar panel is one fixed to the roof because the panel needs to have the best intensity of light and one fixed on the roof only reaches its peak at midday. A moveable panel - either portable or rotating on the roof - can be aimed into the sun ensuring it can convert optimum sunlight into power. One of the best-kept secrets in the motorhoming world is that ex-test solar panels are available in Spain at reduced prices. To find these deals ask fellow motorhomers for the whereabouts of Bert - a Dutch man who sells and installs the panels and various other items. Many motorhomers know him and visit him regularly at free-parks in Southern Spain during the winter. To understand better the worth of solar panels visit www.motorhomefacts.com where there is a solar calculator to work out how much power a panel will generate. Our personal view is that we would not fit a solar panel but then we would not free-park in one place for weeks on end either.

Wind generators

Have similar issues to solar panels and indeed can be run in conjunction with them, however you may become a slave to electricity generation. They do have the best potential for electricity up to 30 amps a day in windy conditions, running 24 hours. The biggest problem is securely fixing them. Pegging them out on the ground is difficult and contravenes the rules of setting up camp when you are entitled only to stop at the side of the road. Some people fix them to the rear of their motorhomes but complain they are noisy at night. Where are you going to store it when on the move? How easy is it to assemble?

Generators

Generators have become a much more affordable option and are available from a variety of sources including DIY stores and supermarkets. Many American motorhomes already have generators fitted. These will recharge your batteries and enable you to watch endless TV without mains electricity. They need to filled with fuel so you have to budget for that. Storage for both the generator and fuel is likely to be a problem and will be a heavy addition. Generators are very antisocial and should not be used at night. Campsites rarely allow generator use. Very few motorhomers have generators, and they are realistically only beneficial when free-parking in one place for a considerable length of time or possibly whilst skiing using camper-stops. Barry and Margaret, of www.magbaztravels.com, told us they had removed their fixed generator to obtain more locker space. Our personal view is generators are simply unnecessary and take up too much space and payload. Nova Leisure produce a chassis mounted gas generator, it is relatively quiet but expensive. One nice feature is that warmed air, a by-product of cooling the generator, is ducted into the motorhome. Tel: 01604 780022 or visit www.novaleisure.com for details.

Fuel cells

Are available from www.Translesure.co.uk Tel: 0113 2522900

costing £2200 including fitting. Although light, economical and virtually silent are realistically just too expensive at the moment equating to 146 nights plugged in at a campsite charging £15 per night.

Gas

There are four items that run on gas within the motorhome: the fridge, hob / cooker and gas fire are standard items. Gas also heats the water. Gas is both extremely flammable and can be explosive. As with electricity correct safety procedures need to be followed, regular servicing undertaken by a qualified person and general vigilance all the time when gas is present.

Types of gas

There are two gasses: Butane and Propane both are types of LPG liquid petroleum gas. The most important difference is operating temperature. Butane will not change from liquid to gas below 0°C, whereas Propane can operate down to -40°C. Butane is heavier than Propane; therefore, 7 and 6kg bottles are the same size as are 13 and 15kg bottles respectively.

Gas bottles

Calor Gas bottles or any other British traditional bottle brands cannot be exchanged or refilled on the continent. Thankfully BP has introduced 10kg and 5kg GRP bottles called BP Gaslite which uses a fibreglass material developed for fighter plane fuel tanks. These bottles have three advantages: they are clear so liquid level can be seen; two 5kg bottles are 10kg lighter than the Calor equivalents and a pair of 10kg save 16kg. A reassuring factor is that they are safer in a fire situation as they melt rather than explode. Bottles can be exchanged in Austria, Belgium, Denmark, Finland, Netherlands, Norway and Sweden. Other countries joining are France and Poland; and more countries are likely to join the scheme. BP say regulators, valve types and occasionally the cylinder colour may vary across Europe but the English version has a 27mm clip-on fitting. The 5kg bottles are 393mm high and 305mm wide and the 10kg are 587mm by 305mm respectively. Few British motorhomes will be able to use these due to the width but they should fit in continental motorhomes and some caravans. A web link is available to confirm and buy individual country adaptors giving specification and provides information about the location of exchange stations www.bpgaslight.co.uk

Although Campingaz is sold in numerous European countries, it is impractical due to its small 2.7kg size. There have been steps to standardise gas systems. Motorhomes and caravans purchased new from 2003 have been fitted with a standardised 30 mbar regulator. Unfortunately, as with BP, the bottle attachments are not standardised so different attachments will still be needed. Gaslow sell a range of adaptors suitable for most European bottles, www.gaslow.co.uk Tel: 01509 843331.

Regulators and Hose Tails

Every country has its own market leader, the equivalent of Calor Gas, the result is that the bottle connections vary widely. As with BP Gaslite, different regulators or hose tails will be required, depending where you buy a new bottle. There is some interchange but the easiest way is to buy the appropriate regulator or hose tail with the bottle. *The Caravan Club Europe* Guides have some individual country information. Gaslow will be able to supply most European regulators and tails.

How many bottles

This all depends on how long you wish to travel, what time of year, how often you intend to use mains electricity and the size of your gas locker. Most British motorhomes accommodate 2 x 6/7kg bottles. Most continental motorhomes accommodate 2 x 11kg bottles, but a 6/7kg and a 13/15kg bottle will normally fit. If you only intend to visit one country, especially if you intend to visit the same country year after year, purchasing a foreign bottle and appropriate attachment/regulator is cost effective and sensible. Motorhomers report that Spain has affordable gas bottles and that autogas is very hard to come by, although Repsol garages are a good place to try, visit www.repsolypf.com

Based on our records, motorhomes on tour during warm months using electricity a third of the time will use one 11kg bottle a month. Our gas was used for hot water, cooking and refrigeration but the fridge was switched over when hooked up or driving. On campsites their showers and sinks were always used. To get round the exchange problem we used an 11kg LPG refillable bottle, bought from TB Turbo. We had a 1993 German motorhome running at 50 mbar. Using the German regulator and an adapter also from TB Turbo we could swap between the refillable and an 11kg German bottle. Exchange of German bottles is possible in a variety of countries (German motorhomers always know where).

During six months wintering in the United Kingdom from September to February, with use of showers, washing machine, a dual electric water heater, electric fan heater, and kettle only two 11kg gas bottles were used.

In one month visiting ski resorts with temperatures ranging from 0°C to 21°C, without electric hook up, expect to use one 11kg bottle a week. In these temperatures a refillable bottle and a spare bottle is the most convenient.

When to exchange

It is useful to know how much gas is in your bottle so an exchange can be planned. The level of gas can be indicated when condensation clings to the bottle. Pouring warm water down the side of the bottle can produce a distinctive temperature difference, also stick on level indicators can be used when the gas is in operation. Alternatively you can weigh the bottle, German bottles have weights down the side and Calor Gas bottles mark the empty weight (curiously in pounds) on the aluminium collar. Probably the easiest way is to buy a regulator with a gauge attached available from various outlets. Automatic changeover units are nice to have but far from a necessity. We have only used our reserve bottle when topping up our refillable one.

Refillable bottles

A range of companies now sell refillable bottles in various sizes, including TB Turbo www.tb-turbo.co.uk Tel: 01524 67157, Gaslow www.gaslow.co.uk Tel: 01509 843331 and MTH Gas Systems Limited www.mthautogas.co.uk Tel: 01594 563538. These provide a solution to the cylinder exchange and adaptor problem as well as saving considerable amounts on gas costs, without the expense of having a fixed tank added. The danger associated with these bottles, especially the early ones, was the lack of cut off valve designed to stop bottles being filled beyond 80 per cent capacity. Filling beyond this point increases the risk of liquid gas passing through the regulator, which then expands approximately 50 times from its liquid state, leading to a significantly increased flame. MTH Gas Systems Limited range (see photo below) includes a lightweight Kevlar refillable bottle. Although on sale the Kevlar bottle is presently without an 80 per cent cut off valve.

LPG availability

There should be no problem filling a fixed tank abroad but a refillable gas bottle may be refused. We have refilled it in England, France, Norway, Sweden, Italy, Bulgaria, Netherlands, and Romania. It helps if you have the correct filling attachment on before you get to the fuel station. The continental fitting is available from TB Turbo, Gaslow, C.A.C tanks and Autogas 2000. The secret is to refill before the gas level becomes low, they can be topped up at any point. A standard auto fill point can be fitted to the outside of your gas locker or sidewall, assuming it is fitted correctly by a suitably qualified gas fitter it should perform like a fixed tank. We would not fit a fixed tank. The gas locker on our

Swift only housed two 4.5kg bottles; it would be far more cost-effective to have this locker enlarged to house a refillable. When you come to sell simply keep your refillable, or sell it separately.

LPG is difficult to obtain in Spain, Greece, Germany and Scandinavia (where you have to be careful not to fill up with natural gas). Details of LPG availability across Europe are found at http://stations.gpl.online.fr.

Safety

Gas is highly flammable and heavier than air. Gas bottles should always be turned off in transit. Vents in the well of the gas locker must never be covered or blocked with mud or snow. Gas bottles must be transported and used in a secure upright position as liquid gas could pass through the regulator resulting in a very big flame. Suspected gas leaks should always be investigated fully using soapy water before appliances are used. Gas leaks on ferries are potentially catastrophic, as gas sinks to the lowest point creating a potentially explosive atmosphere. Therefore gas systems should be fully turned off before embarkation.

Water systems

Motorhomes can have three separate systems: fresh water, dirty water from sinks and showers called grey water/waste and toilet waste called black waste/water.

Fresh water

Motorhomes generally have a fixed fresh water tank, normally located internally. A secure integral fresh tank is advised when free-parking and essential in sustained freezing conditions. On campsites it is nice to have a tank that does not need filling daily. And increasingly, fully serviced pitches allow constant fresh water. A tank that holds less than 100 litres is not sufficient for those intending to free-park.

Water is heavy, one litre weighing one kilo. Some motorhomers discard fresh water before departing. This is fine if you know exactly where you are going but inadvisable if you don't. It is sensible to keep enough for a night, in case water is not available when you arrive or you are late.

Water economics

An evaluation of our water usage averages 20 litres a day for drinks, washing up and other essentials. If you shower another 30 litres, 15 each, should be adequate. Two strip washes used ten litres maximum. Washing in the hand washing machine uses 20 litres of water. Giving an average daily total of 20-70 litres. With strict water conservation it is possible to use less than 20 litres a day, but far easier to use more than 100 litres. We never ran out of water (110 litre tank) our longest stop was four nights without refill but still had 30 litres remaining.

When gathering free-park information from other motorhomers, always ask if water is available. Those using camper-stops and free-parks on an 'as we find them' basis generally travel with tanks at least three quarters full, so it is possible to stay a few days. Many experienced free-parking motorhomers carry a full tank of water and extra 20 litre containers at the expense of other items.

Filling the tank

Fresh water tanks normally have an outside filler point, which looks similar to the fuel cap. Many campsites and camper-stops have areas designed for motorhomes to dump and restock with water. A short length of food quality hose with a tap connection is quick to attach and easy to store. Water tanks located under seats or between floor layers usually have a large inspection/filler hole making filling easy. Plastic watering cans are popular for keeping tanks topped up. Whatever you intend to use ensure it is food quality as plastic items, especially hoses, can cause a TCP taste.

Purification

Water quality varies and can appear a little dubious, even when marked 'potable'. Bottled drinking water is cheap and widely available from shops but costly on space, weight and convenience. Drinking water is available in campsites and most towns, hopefully marked 'potable', sometimes identified by seeing people filling drinking bottles. It may have a cloudy appearance and a chemical taste. It is possible to use water purification tablets. A water filter is most convenient and are relatively easy to fit, but are not cheap.

Some claim to provide protection from nasty tastes and bacteria. There are many on the market and it is important to obtain a suitable filter not simply for taste. Depending on the length of the trip, refill cartridges will need to be carried.

Hot water

An electric heater element in the hot water tank is great but is unlikely to be worth retro fitting except for those regularly wintering. Boiling a kettle and using the shower block is cost effective.

Solar shower - This is a black plastic sack with a shower head coming off it, available from outdoor shops and Argos. Basically you fill it with water and leave it out in the sun all day to heat up. On very hot days the water can heat to extreme temperatures and cold water will need to be added before use. Excellent for those on a budget or free-parking, it can also be used for storing extra non drinking water.

Waste systems

Grey waste

Refers to dirty water from sinks and shower. Grey water is either collected in a fixed tank often mounted under floor or an outside portable container. External tanks' contents will freeze in sustained freezing conditions, which is only a problem if you shower, as all other activities can be carried out in a washing up bowl and disposed of appropriately. An electric element can be added to grey waste tanks to prevent freezing. Having one fitted would be pointless unless you are going skiing for two weeks or more and not staying on a campsite. Disposing of grey water is easy at a motorhome dump. Some campsites ask you to drain out onto plants that seem to thrive on it, though due to the food content this can be stinky. It is best to avoid liquids such as oils, starchy water and hazardous waste being discarded into this tank. Pouring diluted bicarbonate of soda occasionally down the drains helps to keep the tank clean and reduces smells.

Black waste

Black waste has to be disposed of responsibly as it poses a health risk. It is not advisable to discard this waste in toilets as the solids, especially paper, tend to block the system. Many campsites, due to remote locations, have septic tank waste systems. Toilet 'blue' chemicals often contain formaldehyde amongst other ingredients, these effectively kill the bacteria that make the septic tank function. Using environmentally friendly 'green' chemicals or a SOG systems are suitable alternatives.

SOG toilet

Designed for built-in cassette style toilets. A small fan vents smells outside when the toilet is in use therefore no chemical is needed. This system is more efficient at controlling toileting smells than proprietary chemicals, as a constant airflow is drawn through the toilet bowl. In a small space this is very welcome especially when sharing the motorhome with less than intimate friends. This system is relatively easy to fit if you have basic 12v electrical knowledge and contortionist arms. A SOG system is definitely good value for money and we will fit one on our next motorhome. This ultimate environmentally friendly system cuts out the weight, space, cost and need of chemical. Concentrated chemical also stains everything it comes in contact with. The only negative of a SOG is vented smells may be directed to your neighbours or 'worse still' into your awning. Contact Symonspeed Ltd Tel: 01803 214602

Dumping grey and black waste

Getting rid of waste is relatively easy and can be done at campsites and camper-stops. When touring dump at every opportunity, regardless of tank levels, as your next stop may not have dumping facilities. Some campsites charge you to dump if you only stay one night, always read the small print. The camper-stop guides detail sani stations and stops with dumps, so you can plan a route to visit one.

On a campsite it is inconvenient to pack up and move just to dump. Motorhomes with a cassette or porta potti system can walk waste to the disposal point then use the cassette for transporting grey as well. Curiously grey water leaves a smell in the tank that cannot be rinsed away. Those with fixed black tanks have to take the motorhome to the dump unless on a suitably serviced pitch.

When plumbed into a waste system the tank must still be used and periodically emptied. Leaving the drain valve open will result in a build up of solids in the tank. Attempting to use a bucket to empty a fixed tank, will almost certainly cause an agricultural outcome, and is definitely antisocial for neighbours. Campsites that don't have a motorhome dump, also called a motorhome service point, usually have a drain-cover that can be lifted, but it is best to ask on arrival. Many camper-stops are suitable for these units.

Dumping (whilst free-parking)

Warning! This section contains the realities some people will not want to know, so if you're not going to free-park move onto further information.

All motorhomers represent the motorhoming community. Free-parking motorhomers need to be particularly responsible, especially when it comes to disposing of toilet waste. Dumping a toilet full of chemicals and waste in the countryside is environmentally unfriendly, unnecessary and probably against the law in every country. It is not always possible to dispose of waste as regularly as you'd like. The following options all have their merits:

Two toilet cassettes: Carrying a spare toilet cassette in an outside locker is particularly favoured by German motorhomers. Cassettes are relatively expensive, bulky and weigh about 25kg when full. Fiamma produce a Porta Kassett designed to carry the spare toilet cassette underneath the motorhome.

Liquids only: By limiting the toilet to urine only, not even toilet paper, will increase the time before emptying, also the emptying experience is less hideous. We also use this technique when on campsites simply because of the emptying experience and only a tiny drop of chemical is required. Public toilets or the bag technique can be used to deal with solid waste.

The bag technique: Use bags for your solid waste including toilet tissue. Incidentally bags specially designed to hold in place in Thetford toilet bowls are available in German camping shops. Disposal in communal wheelie bins that are available all over Europe, ensures waste is dealt with safely as they are also used for nappies and sanitary wear. Save lidded jars for this waste when immediate disposal is unavailable, sauerkraut jars are particularly suitable. Carrier bags work well, but always check for holes! We recommend having a pee before attempting this option and advise that toilet paper is put in the bag, just in case. Some people have not worked out responsible toileting and disappear into the bushes with a roll of paper ch-ch-ch-charming!

The bottle technique: To further reduce liquid in the toilet men can re-fill lidded bottles and discard the waste in the bin or down a toilet when available.

Flushing: Flush for as short a time as necessary, when not using the bag technique a couple of well placed sheets of paper whilst keeping the hole open reduces cleaning. When an auto flush is activated by opening the hole this can be controlled by switching the pump off.

Further information on utilities

- John Wickersham's books produced by Haynes the Motorcaravan / Caravan Manual or Caravan Handbook are essential, explaining all utilities and their component parts in great detail.
- Basic information on electrics can be found in Caravan Club Europe guides

Chapter 4 - Preparing your Motorhome

There are so many gadgets and gismos it is difficult to know what to add to your motorhome and it is easy to get carried away. France, Germany and Italy all have large accessory shops and motorhome shows so don't feel you have to buy everything before you go. If you're not certain you need it, don't take it; remember your motorhome weight limits.

Security

Security of the motorhome and personal safety must take top priority. Having the motorhome broken into, or worse, stolen, would be hideous. In reality all you can do is secure the motorhome, making it as unattractive as possible to criminals.

'Security of the motorhome and personal safety must take top priority'

Alarms

There are many alarms available, from simple movement sensor alarms, looking similar to a smoke alarm, to sophisticated integrated systems. See viewpoint on page 60 for a description of a benchmark alarm system.

Gas alarms

This device can detect a leak from your gas system and gasses used to anaesthetise motorhomers. Engine starting spray is used as it has high ether content, anaesthetising sleeping occupants then robbing the motorhome. Gas attacks are very rare and the fear of them shouldn't ruin your trip. Gas attacks are most commonly reported to happen at motorway service stations in France and Germany, presumably because these are anonymous places, with fast escape routes. There are plenty of excellent campsites and camper-stops in both countries, so there is no need to sleep at service stations. Gas alarms can be fitted independently or integrated into the main alarm system. A gas alarm that detects narcotics, LPG and carbon monoxide is available from Sleep-C-Cure who also produce several good security gadgets and a useful looking window vent www.Sleep-C-Cure.co.uk Tel: 01580 895358.

Safes

The simple rule is, if you don't want to lose it, don't take it with you. Important documents have to be taken and should be protected. No system is foolproof. Delaying or preventing a thief in an opportunist situation is probably the most you can achieve. Various safes are available from DIY superstores and Argos that can fit into floor wells or cupboards. Argos stocks a laptop safe weighing 13kg, also having enough space for all essentials.

Additional locks

A wide range of additional locks and security gadgets are available. Visual physical security is worth adding, as thieves will always target the easiest option. Additional locks for the caravan door are available in several styles, from strong dead locks to ones that act as handles. Remember, if you have a stable door you need to lock both door sections. Fiamma produce a very strong lock but it is possible to lock yourself out and be locked in. A steering wheel lock is sensible. A gas attack reported to us in Germany implied that the thieves had a Fiat master door key. A simple solution is to add a swivelling metal clip that prevents the doorknob rising. These are available from Sleep-C-Cure who also have a similar 'caravan door' solution. Another simple trick is to strap both cab door handles to each other, or use two rear seatbelt straps available from scrap yards that fit in the motorhome belt clips. Sliding window security is improved by cutting a dowel to fit into the channel thereby jamming the window.

To find out the vulnerable parts of your motorhome, pretend to lock your keys inside and ask friends especially agile teenagers to 'break in' with you without causing damage.

Sensor lights

A useful, cheap, relatively easy to fit addition, that enables owners easy access to the motorhome at night and thief deterrent.

Dynamic security

Best described as a trick of the mind, and probably more likely to prevent a robbery than physical deterrents. The little things like:

- Parking in a very visible space rather than an isolated corner
- Putting valuables out of sight
- Tying a dog lead on your bike rack.
- Shutting curtains and blinds so unknown whether in or out.
- Leaving a light or radio on
- Sticking multi language labels on windows explaining that a sophisticated alarm is fitted
- Never leaving keys laying around or on display at any time
- Leaving your dummy wallet out on the side at night so your real one is not searched for.

Treating campsites the same way as free-parks, especially those used when visiting capital cities, stops your motorhome looking vulnerable.

Trackers

Having spent so much on a motorhome these should be good value for money. The key issue is insurance. Generally motorhome insurance is inexpensive, therefore any reduction in premium is unlikely to be more than the annual administration for the tracker.

The second element is the reduced time delay between a motorhome being stolen and recovered by the police. Hopefully the criminals will be caught and any insurance claim settled quicker. Whilst abroad with the vehicle it is down to the owner to liase with the local police and organise the recovery. Personally we have not had a tracker fitted, but these could be considered inexpensive if you have just bought a brand new motorhome. Further information can be sought from Van Bitz. www.vanbitz.com Tel: 01823 321992

Trailers and caravans

Wheel clamps and hitch locks are essential. Some insurance companies insist on these being fitted. Caravan/motorhome leg locks are cheap and effective, their best advantage being small size and weight.

We had a Van Bitz alarm fitted to our Hymer motorhome. Sensors were on external doors, bonnet and every locker except the toilet. A wire loop was added that alarmed the bikes and trailer. An engine immobiliser and internal microwave movement sensor were included. The job was completed in a day and they gave excellent service. A two year component and workmanship warranty is standard. A mobile phone alert should the alarm be triggered is optional. The Strikeback T is an approved Thatcham category alarm. We feel that it was money well spent and helped in getting a good price when we sold the motorhome.

We always set the alarm when unattended, when we were inside at night the microwave movement sensor was switched off leaving the lockers, doors and bike loop alarmed. Of 298 nights away, we spent 123 in camper-stops or free-parks, there was never any evidence of anyone attempting to break in. We opted to have an integrated gas alarm fitted, to use when free-parking also using it on other occasions. Fiamma door locks were fitted; we often locked the bottom half of the stable door when we were inside. Be aware that these should be locked in the open position to prevent occupants being locked into the motorhome. This was our only home and the last thing we wanted to be was homeless, so these gadgets did give us considerable peace of mind.

Safety

Fire extinguisher

An essential item that should be located near but not over the cooker, in very large motorhomes two may be appropriate. Some countries require these to be carried in every road vehicle. These are available from most camping and caravan stockists, the smallest car sized extinguishers are probably insufficient.

Smoke alarm

Smoke alarms designed for caravans, often with a temporary silence function, cost around £20, it would be silly not to have one.

Carbon monoxide alarm

Look and work in a similar way to smoke alarms. A cheap lightweight peace of mind equipment that means you can sleep at night with your gas heater on. See gas alarm above for a three way solution.

Extras and add-ons

Campernalia, an international multi-million pound industry, providing a cacophony of items for your every whim, from self heating food to kitchen sinks. None of these are essential but some are worth considering. These have been prioritised in usefulness for the average motorhomer, but as everyone has different priorities and lifestyles, different things will be important.

Awnings

An awning has a range of uses. They provide additional living and storage space with sun and shower protection, as well as somewhere to dry the washing. There are several types of awning offering different advantages.

Wind out awning: a fixed roof height roller blind. These can be set up in a minute, providing useful shade to keep heat off the motorhome and its occupants. Side panels are available. This type of awning is unsuitable in windy conditions. These regularly get damaged when driving, catching in narrow areas and tight corners. A removable awning is the budget choice. We would add a fixed roll out awning if we were going touring but a 'drive away' awning (see below) is better when wintering.

Drive away awning: Ideal for campsite based motorhomers they often resemble a tent and are free standing, so can be left on the campsite when the motorhome is taken off site. The Doréma Highlander Annex is like a caravan awning available from Towsure Tel: 0870 6090070 www.towsure.co.uk. An extensive range of caravan style awnings are made by Harrison available from Riversway Leisure www.riverswayleisure.co.uk Tel: 01772 729999. They provide sleeping compartments living space or a kitchen. The disadvantage of these is they cannot be used in camper-stops/free-parks, and require valuable storage space and payload.

Fiamma/Omni vent top vent fan and all weather cover

A simple 12v fan retro fitting into the common size top vents that either extracts or impels. Being reasonably quiet and as low as 0.5Ah these are great as cooking/condensation extractors and a better alternative than air conditioning, adding an all weather cover gives total flexibility. For further information see ***Chapter 7***. This is another piece of equipment we would add if going touring or spending long periods in hot climates.

Fly screens

It is of vital importance to secure your motorhome to the number one intruder - the mosquito. Many sleepless nights and itchy days have been lost to the motorhome community across Europe. Every window and vent should have a secure fly screen before it is opened. This material is widely available and can be retro fitted if necessary. The door also needs protection, we retro fitted a Fiamma Moskito Net and found it effective even in Finland where mosquitoes are prolific.

Reversing Camera

These can avoid those annoying accidents, keep an eye on a trailer or provide rear security (with sound). They really do help when reversing if the camera is positioned correctly and the monitor is of a good enough quality. The lens needs regular cleaning in wet conditions, they also suffer condensation and you will become reliant on them. Definitely worth adding.

Cab Window Screens

The cab windows provide very little thermal protection. Screens do provide good insulation, in both very hot and very cold weather, but are only necessary in extreme conditions. Condensation is also alleged to be controlled. There are two types of screen available, internal and external. External screens get wet and dirty, needing to be dried, and cleaned, before storing. Internal screens suffer condensation as soon as outside temperatures cool and inside humidity levels reach 60% and also need drying before storing. Those free-parking or using camper-stops use internal screens. The general rule is park-up ready to go. A better option is the fixed Seitz concertina blinds, these provide adequate insulation and are not bulky to store. Although expensive they allow instant use and privacy without the performance. We would fit these if sufficient curtains were not provided. A well designed curtain system is available from Fiamma.

Chapter 7 Wintering details how to make internal screens cheaply and it may be worth considering this option.

Assisted suspension (air rides)

Should not be necessary but they do significantly improve ride comfort to motorhomes that have boat tendencies. Motorhomes built on AL-KO chassis are unlikely to need this but motorhomes that are wide with long overhangs and scooters probably will. There are safety issues to consider regarding break loading. Altering the ride height could cause the load sensing device to provide un-balanced front and rear breaking. *The Motoraravan Manual* explains the fitting of these with several useful pictures. Whether its worth adding them on a well designed responsibly loaded motorhome is purely down to cost against use during ownership but certainly should not be an excuse for overloading. AL-KO has now started fitting these devices for even better performance.

External storage (mounted storage boxes)

These are widely available in various sizes and can be fixed to the roof or bike rack. These can become the motorhome equivalent of a loft. Realistically only needed on B class motorhomes, where space is limited but spare payload is more likely to be available.

Satellite Navigation

Many motorhomers, especially those that don't map read love this addition. They can save a lot of arguing and stress, they provide pinpoint accuracy, at a fraction of the weight of maps. Do be prepared in case it breaks down. Take a map and attend a map reading course if necessary. Some Satellite Navigation users complain that their system cannot calculate the suitability of the road to the vehicle, so they have found themselves in some surprisingly tight corners. Having said that the navigator in our motorhome has occasional malfunctions. Microsoft AutoRoute can be run on a

Laptop and an GPS receiver can plugged in, providing a bigger screen, one less piece of equipment and has voice prompted directions. Action replay can provide a similar package using Navigator software, www.action-replay.co.uk or Tel: 05511 346245. We've never purchased a navigation system because: how can you be lost if you don't know where you are going?

Www.thewrinklies.co.uk reads: Programmed Mavis [the satellite navigation system] to take us to Eupen and set off. Got to Eupen and she had a brainstorm, forgot we were driving a vehicle 6.5 metre long, 2.5 metres wide and 2.9 metres high. She sent us down this narrow side street, which rapidly turned into an 18% hill (downwards) then we were faced with a concrete bollard in the middle of the road. Tried reversing back up the hill, just made an awful smell from clutch area! I then noticed that I could just get through between the wall and the bollard (after checking that there was clear path to road beyond) All I had to do was move a concrete post that was lying beside the bollard. Grasp end of post firmly and lift - ouch! I discovered that on underside was broken remains of a glass reflector. Sit down with blood pouring from two badly gashed fingers! I don't do blood, especially my own, so it's time for sympathy vote approach again. With handkerchief wrapped around fingers I drove to a nearby factory, after scaring daylights out of lady fireman who had parked her car at the exit end of the lane. Last time she saw a vehicle come down that lane Belgium still used francs!!

Solar panels and generators

If these come with your vehicle they are probably nice to have, but there are questions over their viability. See ***Chapter 3: Utilities.***

Air conditioning/cooling

If you plan to travel to Southern Europe in August then it is worth considering an air conditioning or cooling system, otherwise these are un-necessary. We have had both air conditioning and air coolers (both already fitted) and were hardly ever used. In August on site where air-con was banned, with heat management 37°C was bearable. The main disadvantages are: cannot be used when not hooked up, even 12 volt versions drain batteries quickly, added weight and wind resistance, noisy, very expensive to buy, service and run. Consider Fiamma/Omni vent above.

Satellite dish/television

Top of the list for some, irrelevant for others. See ***Chapter 8: Entertainment.***

Stays (Steadies)

These are legs that can be wound to the ground to stop the motorhome rocking when stationary but the effort of placing them down can outweigh their benefit. Some motorhomers remove them to increase weight capacity. Our stays were put down twice and it was so much effort we didn't bother again.

Silver tyre covers

Some people cover the tyres to prevent cracking and premature ageing. Only necessary when parked up for a long time but it is equally important to move the motorhome forwards or backwards periodically. Tyres over five years old probably need replacing; try a couple of tyre fitters for an expert opinion.

Michelin camping tyres

Are excellent having extra sidewall reinforcement and superior grip compared to ordinary tyres. We would always fit these now when tyres need replacing.

Outside water points

Used for outside showers and hosepipes. Probably more useful for motorhomers with children or animals or warm wintering but far from essential.

Outside gas point

For use with a gas barbeque or cooker. We always barbequed before we toured Europe and invested in a gas barbeque, we used it twice and finally discarded it in Italy. Again more likely to be used if warm wintering with an awning.

Additional Modes of Transport

Depending on how you intend to spend your time abroad affects any additional transport you may require. Most countries have adequate parking areas without height barriers. Of all the motorhomers we meet about 1 per cent have an alternative form of motorised transport.

Bicycle

This is an excellent and cheap mode of transport, ideal for getting around on or off the campsite. Many European towns have bicycle routes and cycling is an excellent way of occupying yourself. Cycle racks are light and relatively unobtrusive, though bikes get dirty no matter how well you cover them. Ideally they need garaging, which means an electric bike could be taken, a lightweight compromise to a scooter. As always payload will decide. In addition, ensure your travel insurance covers any bicycle related accidents. If you have a bike languishing in a shed will you really use it abroad? The Fiamma Carry Bike can hold up to 60 kg. A standard bike weighs around 14 kg. An electric bike weighs 28 kg (including battery pack but not charger).

When a bike rack is used it's worth attaching a hazard square, which is a legal requirement in some countries. It is a square with red and white stripes diagonally across it, available from accessory shops at home and abroad. This seems to appease the authorities in the Mediterranean countries where rear protrusions can be an issue. A permanently fixed bike rack is included when calculating the 60 per cent overhang calculations see ***Wheelbase, overhang and clearance in Chapter 2.***

Scooter/motorcycle

A few motorhomers opt to take a scooter or motorbike. Of the three British couples we met with scooters, one had decided to get rid of it, as they didn't use it, one biker couple frequently used theirs, and one couple occasionally use one but admit to not needing it. Scooters are an expensive option against a bicycle, though few motorhomes have sufficient payload, even some with garages, thus a trailer is necessary. Realistically unless you're an enthusiast the compromises outweigh the benefits. People determined to take a scooter who don't want the additional expense and inconvenience of towing will need to have a scooter rack fitted. Buy with caution as they weigh about 100kg and a scooter weighs at least 70 kg. Ensure the chassis extensions are suitable as we have seen several motorhomes with an obvious bend. PWS Engineering Ltd Tel: 01202 746851, manufacture and fit both towbars and scooter racks. Di Blasi produce a folding scooter, weighing 35 kg, they are unbelievably easy to fold and erect, visit www.concept-edge.co.uk Tel: 01895850455. A permanently fixed scooter rack is included in calculating the 60 per cent overhang see ***Wheelbase, overhang and clearance Chapter 2.***

Cars

Towing a car is in complete contradiction to the spirit of motorhoming. This statement is not made lightly and the following example speaks for itself.

Suitable motorhome parking is widely available on the continent, public transport is easy to use and even when we were static on campsites getting around was easy. The car did not outweigh the inconvenience of towing and extra cost of insurance, tax, fuel, tolls, ferries and campsite charges.

Fitting a tow bar reduces the motorhome payload by at least 30 kg. Licence holders restricted to towing 750 kg will have to purchase a micro car or take a further driving test. Axiam www.axaim.co.uk and Ligier www.ligier.es are two manufacturers of sub 750kg micro cars. Visit www.micro-cars.co.uk for more information. Another alternative is the qpod, weighing as little as 220kg. Visit www.uniquemotorcompany.co.uk Tel: 0870 2414804. The qpod is designed to be a 'trailer' in its own right, this is discussed in the *'trailer or A-frame'* section below.

With our 27' 8.23m American motorhome we felt stranded without an additional mode of transport but towing the Cinquecento made journeys difficult.

Believing we would move from place to place, using the car to discover the local area, we purchased a smaller motorhome, an Aixam micro car and 750 kg rated trailer. Our diary Day Two, 'The Dutch are fascinated by our little car, they keep staring at it. They also think our camper is very big, not how we expected them to react at all.' After four months and 12144 kilometres the Aixam and trailer were abandoned in France, as the car simply wasn't used or subsequently missed.

A couple that lived in a very large American motorhome, who had previously owned a car, opted to rent a car when required. They took their motorhome out for the day once a week, combining dumping, shopping and sightseeing. In ***Chapter 1 'The Motorhome Reality'***, we described a situation where a car was needed with the result that the motorhome was abandoned.

Towing - trailer or A-frame

There are two options, a trailer or the A-frame system. The A-frame system is a convenient simple solution once the car is adapted. A simple frame is attached to the car then hooked up like any other trailer. Although this system is not illegal in this country, as long as trailer rules are complied with, this may bring unnecessary police attention to you in countries where it is unusual. It is almost impossible to reverse when an A-framed car is attached. Those still interested should contact PRO-Tow Frames, manufacturers of CAR-A-TOW, visit www.protowframes.co.uk or Tel: 01202 632456. Towing a car on a trailer is legal everywhere. Box trailers provide a self contained, lockable storage area suitable for free-parkers, or long term site users who want to transport additional items. The qpod micro car gets around the issues of trailers and A-frames, fitting a towing bar converts the vehicle into a trailer as the front wheels are completely off the road whilst being towed. More details on the qpod is detailed in *'Cars'* above.

Whenever towing, licence and weight restrictions must be observed also consider additional driver's abilities and licences. Many motorhome manufacturers recommend surprisingly low towing capacities normally due to chassis extensions. Confirm this, as they are likely to be less than the figure stamped on the chassis manufacturers weight specification plate.

A typical motorhome basic inventory

The Motorhome inventory chart details the weights of items typically found in motorhomes. This is by no means a definitive list but does give an idea of the sort of things you should consider carrying before any luxuries, hobbies or mementoes.

ITEM	APPROX WEIGHT
SPARES, REPAIRS AND SERVICING - OILY BITS!	**KG**
Screwdrivers, spanners, socket set	5kg
Hammer, chisel, pliers	3kg
Hacksaw full size (can be used to trim low branches)	520g
Light weight hand or cordless drill and bits	1kg
Second jack, capable of jacking laden motorhome, as vehicle jack often not good enough	5kg
Tow rope/hawser, jump leads	1.5kg
Appropriate sealant (bathroom sealant, aluminium/caravan sealant) and gun	1kg
Gaffer tape (use with caution as difficult to remove- excellent to repair silver screens and bike covers).	300g
WD40, Oil, lubricants and grease	300g
Workshop manual of base vehicle - useful for fixing the problem or showing people abroad what the problem is.	
Two boxes nuts/bolts/glues/tapes and other things you may need including: Batteries (various), instant gasket, PTFE/electrical tape , Bolt and padlock set for emergency door/locker security, Bungees, sewing kit, glue - wood and plastic, Bulbs, fuses - domestic and auto, Plugs - UK and adaptor plus fuses, Jubilee clips, zip ties - various sizes, Various screws, nuts and bolts, washers, Gloves - latex and strong workman's style, overalls, Alan keys, tape measure, stanley knife, 12v soldering iron, electrical multi metre	5 kg
ESSENTIAL EQUIPMENT	**KG**
In date first aid kit	500g
Smoke / carbon monoxide alarms	125g each
Fire extinguisher	1.8kg
Two warning triangles	1kg
High visibility vest for every passenger,	100g
Spare bulb and fuse Kits	100g
Euro number plates or GB sticker	10g
A spare pair of glasses (if you wear them)	100g
All but smoke / carbon monoxide alarms are legally required in most countries.	

ADD-ONS AND EXTRAS	KG
Fiamma door locks	1kg
Wind out awning 190 Fiamma/Omnister	5.3/5.5kg
Wind out awning 360 Fiamma/350 Omnister	12.2/13kg
CAMPSITE/PARKING	**KG**
Spirit level	30g
Levelling chocks - two minimum, those on campsites might consider three or four	1.5kg each
Step (extra one may be necessary)	400g
Fresh water carrying container 20L	980g
Awning pegs (if applicable)	800g
A torch: mini maglite/large rechargeable torch	100g/1.04kg
25 metre electric hook up cable	5kg
Leisure plug to domestic plug UK/continental	600g
Money belt	30g
Safe	13kg
Steering lock	5kg
Plastic bristle door mat outside use (very light easily shaken clean and dry)	330g
1x camping chair per person, but make sure it is comfortable	4kg
1x camping table if dinette not freestanding	4kg
1x wind break	4kg
Floor mat for awning when visiting Mediterranean campsites as pitches are normally sandy or dusty	1kg per linear metre
CLEANING PRODUCTS (AVAILABLE ACROSS EUROPE)	**KG**
Firm bristled brush: essential for brushing dirt off shoes, washing camper, brushing out camper floor and carpets	160g
Upholstery/carpet stain remover: essential for removing red wine and tea.	400g
Bicarbonate of soda - washing food, deodorising fridge and various other uses including toothpaste and indigestion cure.	400g
Vinegar - Stain and lime scale remover, surface cleaner which is non abrasive. Also used to repel ants and treat insect bites/stings.	500g
Toilet seal lubricant spray, olive oil can be used but not Vaseline or grease as they soften rubber	250g

KITCHEN EQUIPMENT	KG
2x cutlery sets per person	300g
1x melamine/plastic dinner plate, lunch plate, bowl, side plate per person	710g
2x cups/mugs per person (1 plastic, 1 china)	260g
2x wooden spoons/1x spatula	100g
1x Tefal sauté pan £19.99 from Argos. This pan is ideal for motorhoming, as it is possible to fry, cook cakes, roast and a variety of one pot wonders.	1.5kg
1x non-stick saucepan /2 tier steamer	0.6kg/1.45kg
Plastic bowl (for salads etc)	140g
Plastic containers for storing Tea bags, leftovers and other items, take away containers are ideal but don't last long.	200g (for 6)
1x glass per person though glasses are available in continental supermarkets with relish or pickles inside.	140g
1x Washing up bowl also hand washing and transporting of washing to line, transporting washing up to campsite sinks, and washing in when necessary (those without a bathroom may wish to take two bowls)	350g
1x tin opener	190g
1x bottle opener	450g
1x chopping board	480g
2x chopping knifes and 1x bread knife	225g
1x plastic measuring jug for cooking, making cocktails and assisting with washing	110g
1x lighter/box of matches	30g
Gas whistling kettle	175g
4 cup stainless steel Tea pot (Tea bag economy)	470g
Scissors	60g
CONSUMABLES	**KG**
Tin of Heinz beans	485g
Jam	625g
Coffee 100g jar	380g
Tea Bags 240	800g
1 Litre UHT milk	1.07kg
Bottle of wine	1.3kg
Bottle champagne	1.65kg

Spirits 1L	1.48kg
1 Litre empty bottle scotch (hic)	505g
4 cans beer	800g
Washing up liquid	135g
Curry powder (plastic pot)	560g
Patikas Tikka Paste (Jar)	520g
Box of eggs	380g
Loaf of bread	750g
1 L bottle of olive oil	1.4kg
Condiments	300g
ELECTRICAL ITEMS	**KG**
1x electric travel kettle or low wattage kettle	750g
1x electric cooking ring Remoska mini oven	1.94kg
1x thermostatic 1/2kw fan heater/cooler	2kg
LAUNDRY ITEMS	**KG**
Clothes pegs (20)	100g
Market clips (used on stalls to secure tarpaulins on)	90g each
Several metres of washing line	90g
A washing carousel	145g
A wonder wash /electric washing machine	1.5/5kg
Universal sink plug	
LINEN	**KG**
A duvet and cover (double)/sleeping bag	8.5g
A pillow and case per person	1.2kg
A sheet (double)	460g
BATHROOM ESSENTIALS	**KG**
A bath towel per person	710g
Shower shoes per person	200g
Wash bag and washing items ideally with handle or ability to be hung on hook (male/female)	960g/1.2kg
Bathrobe/dressing gown per person	740g
Solar shower (if using camper-stops/farm sites)	300g
Environmental toilet products 1.5L (toilet green/rinse)	1.7kg
Toilet roll (Andrex)	170g

ALL WEATHER CLOTHES	KG
Umbrella	
Waterproof jacket per person (pac-a-mac style)	600g
Walking shoes/boots	1.85kg
Slip on shoes for easy exit from motorhome and around camp - ideally clogs or welly shoes that can be used in all weather	505g
PAPER WORK	**KG**
Accounts book to log finances	100g
Calculator	40g
Pens	50g
Original /duplicate paperwork	760g
Binoculars - for reading road signs	300g
EXTRAS FOR WINTERERS	**KG**
Mini electric oven/grill	3kg
Drive away awning or sided gazebo	18-24kg
Second electric heater for awning	2kg
Light to use in awning	1.2kg
Electric blanket	1.6kg
BOOKS	**KG**
The Motorhome Manual or Caravan Handbook - John Wickersham, Haynes	810g
The Caravan Club Europe Guides	1.6kg
Camper Stop Guides; Reise Mobile's Bord Atlas, Le Guide National des Aires De Service, Plein Air's Portolano per Camper E Caravan	1.38kg
Discount campsite guides; Camping Card ACSI booklet, Camping Cheque Site Directory, Information Camping Card International	1.1kg
Tourist Information	600g
Tourist Guides	
5 paperback books to read for leisure (remember book swapping is encouraged)	1.07kg
Michelin Europe Road Map (detailed country maps for France, Italy and Germany each weigh the same)	760g
MMM (Magazine)	750g
Motor caravan (Magazine)	445g
Practical Motorhome (Magazine)	460g
Which Motor caravan (Magazine)	480g

LEISURE ITEMS	KG
1000 Ti portable generator (Dry)	14kg
Solar Panel 80w	7.9g
14" TV (12v and 12v)	8kg
15" LCD TV	4kg
DVD player	1.3kg
Maxview crank-up satellite system (dish)	10kg
Inverter	1-2kg
Electric bike	28kg
De Blasi folding bike	14.2kg
De Blasi folding scooter	35kg
Scooter	70kg (from)
Fiamma ultra box 360 (back box)	14kg
Fiamma ultra box (top box)	10-17kg

Based on this chart, essential equipment for two people weighs a minimum of 150kg and includes; bedding, awning, tools, campsite equipment, laundry, kitchen, bathroom, camping equipment and books. Personal luggage (clothes and shoes) for two people is 50 kg plus 40 kg of consumables including food and drink all adding up to 240 kg. This does not include any hobby equipment, laptop, TV or satellite. Allowance of 100kg per additional passenger including luggage should be available. No additional form of transport has been added - no bicycles, or scooters. Those travelling in the UK, with good recovery package, could consider taking considerably less tools. These weights are advisory only. Everyone is advised to weigh his or her loaded motorhome to ensure it is not overloaded.

Accessory shops

Just because you have a motorhome doesn't mean you have to purchase everything from camping shops, other sources are listed below. There are a wealth of camping shops in Europe, especially France, Germany and Italy. If you're not sure about something try living without it and if you don't use it give it away, sell it or send it back to the UK.

Road Pro: A supplier of all things electrical. www.roadpro.co.uk

Towsure: A camping store with a mail order service, offering a wide range of products. Tel 0870 60 900 70 www.towsure.co.uk or visit their stores in Southampton, Birmingham or Sheffield.

Riversway leisure: A camping store with mail order catalogue www.riverswayleisure.co.uk Tel: 01772 729999

www.Amazon.co.uk: Try this site for travel guides, and don't forget that Camper-stop guides are available from www.amazon.fr for France and www.amazon.de for Germany

O'leary Motorhomes: Offer a range of products. Visit www.olearymotorhomes.co.uk Tel: 01482 868632

C.A.K Tanks: Predominantly water products, also a good range of accessories. Tel: 0870 7572324 www.caktanks.co.uk

Argos: Have camping accessories, including awnings, water bottles and toys including snorkelling accessories, kites, etc.

£ Shops: Often lightweight alternatives are available.

Chapter 5 - Paperwork

Although it would be lovely to pack the bags and go, there is some administration that should be done before departure, ensuring your time away runs as smoothly as possible.

Keeping Legal

There is not complete harmonisation for automotive law in Europe, therefore a vehicle compliant with the laws of the registered country is accepted as a temporary visitor. This means your motorhome should be taxed, insured, with a valid MOT and complies with all other UK legislation. Headlights will need to be adjusted to prevent other motorists being dazzled and the road rules of each country observed.

MOT

An MOT is a vehicle inspection of roadworthiness, carried out by an appropriately approved vehicle inspection tester to the standards laid down by the Ministry of Transport. It is not possible to get an MOT abroad and equivalent tests are not accepted. If you are planning to be away when your vehicle either requires its first or annual renewal you will have to return to the UK. An MOT is not required for three years from the date of first registration i.e. until it is three years old and then annually thereafter. A vehicle can be MOT'd at any time whether or not the current one has expired. A vehicle can be MOT'd up to 31 days before expiry of the current MOT so the new MOT starts as the existing expires, therefore 13 months MOT is achieved.

Road vehicle licence (tax disc)

Every UK road registered vehicle must display a valid tax disc when on the public highway. You are required to keep a valid tax disc displayed on your motorhome while you travel in Europe. Concessionary rates apply, for confirmation contact either the DVLA or post office. Tax discs can be applied for two months in advance, providing a six or twelve month licence. The DVLA will send it to you whilst you are away as long as you have a valid MOT, which you would need to send to them along with your insurance certificate. This is inconvenient if you wish to keep driving your motorhome while you await your tax disc, as vital paperwork has to be sent away. If your motorhome MOT and tax disc do not expire on the same month, you can surrender the tax disc to the DVLA during the month you have you motorhome MOT'd. The DVLA will refund the value of each whole month and you can purchase a new tax disc thus adjusting any imbalance between MOT and road tax.

Vehicle insurance

Adequate insurance for every vehicle must be obtained before you travel. Many companies offer insurance for trips of 60, 90 and 180 days. Some companies offer insurance policies designed for cars, so check whether awnings are protected and how much contents insurance is included, realistically this needs to be at least £3,000. Try The Caravan Club, The Camping and Caravan Club and Saga also check for adverts in magazines.

Always check the small print and confirm that the following is insured:

- The motorhome will be driven home if you are incapable of driving it
- That the help line is 24-hours, 365 days a year
- That an alternative motorhome or accommodation is offered in the event of an accident or loss
- That a bail bond is offered in Spain should the vehicle be impounded after an accident
- Which countries are covered, usually these are EU countries, and how you get green cards for additional countries.
- What happens if you break down? Are roadside repairs undertaken or are you simply towed to the nearest garage?
- What factors invalidate your insurance?

Remember that travelling without a current tax disc and MOT will probably invalidate your insurance but you should be able to avoid this situation if you follow our recommendation of travelling in four month blocks.

180 days should be enough for most motorhomers but Bakers of Cheltenham Tel: 0800 4961516 www.towergategroup.co.uk or Comfort www.comfort-insurance.co.uk Tel: 020 8984 0777 offer insurance for those who wish to go full time.

Foreign nationals buying a motorhome in the UK should visit www.downunderinsurance.co.uk who offer motorhome insurance for the UK and Europe to Australians, Americans, Canadians, New Zealanders and South Africans and Brits over 40. They offer cover to people 20 years or older, the registered owner of the vehicle, up to four named drivers and a domestic/social and pleasure owner. They also offer cover if the vehicle is not older than 32 years, free from major modification to the motor or body, and must have less than seven seats. Call free from UK landlines and phone boxes on Tel: 0800 393908.

Recovery

Buying motorhome recovery is not as straightforward as it is for a private car, there are issues at home, which could be exaggerated whilst abroad. Some insurance policies also include adequate recovery. When buying recovery it is imperative to check that the level of UK and European breakdown supplied suits your needs, some policies only arrange for the vehicle to be taken to the nearest garage. Even if you primarily intend to use your motorhome in the United Kingdom, breakdown recovery for larger vehicles may become an issue. It is important that you clearly detail the size and weight of your motorhome to your recovery provider ensuring they can and will recover your motorhome, you may wish to have this confirmed in writing.

Motorhome recovery is often difficult, due to weight and the rear overhang. The overhang prevents towing on a hydraulic lift system where the front wheels are lifted off the ground, as the rear of the motorhome could get damaged. Instead a special vehicle designed for recovering lorries may have to be used. Ridged or rope systems may be suitable for a short distance as long as the towing vehicle is sufficiently large. Automatic vehicles cannot be towed unless the drive wheels are off the road. Some recovery companies will not recover vehicles they deem to be overweight.

The worst-case scenario is breaking down, not being able to speak the language, with no mobile phone signal, somewhere you probably shouldn't have been. We free parked in an isolated Bulgarian village, on a small mountain road. We awoke in the morning to find the market had set up, though kindly left enough space for us to get out. The temperature had dropped to -21°C overnight, and hadn't risen. Our gas regulator was struggling to let enough gas through and we were keen to get going. When the key was turned the engine showed sluggish signs of life but wouldn't start. We quickly realised it was nothing we could fix but what could we do? The bonnet was removed and jump leads attached before a retreat into the motorhome which was only slightly warmer than outside. We soon became the talk of the village and drew a crowd including the police and army. International sign language from the market holders informed us they had called a mechanic. The mechanic needed our vehicle at his garage so a large truck was found somewhere and we were towed down the road. At the garage our fuel filter was replaced, a condensation build up had frozen and our battery needed replacing. We were jump started and given directions to the nearest town and battery fitter. When we arrived they were waiting for us and within five minutes had fitted the correct battery. It all cost £70 and not a word of English was spoken. Never underestimate human kindness.

Personal insurance

Personal insurance is not a legal requirement but inadvisable to travel without it. Independent motorhomers should remember there is no tour rep or travel company support. Ensure your insurance provides at least the following:

- Fly you home if medically required
- Fly out relatives if you are ill or imprisoned
- Repatriate your body
- Provide search and rescue
- Provide adequate medical cover. Those with existing medical conditions can still obtain insurance from All Clear to Travel www.allcleartravel.co.uk Tel: 0870 7779339 or Free Spirit Travel

Insurance www.free-spirit.com Tel: 0845 230 5000. It may be worth visiting www.travelhealth.co.uk which details other possible insurers.

- Provide cover for sports and activities - such as bicycling, swimming, travelling in someone else's car. In addition check whether activities you might embark on such as horse riding, skiing, windsurfing, canoeing or dangerous sports are covered if required. Be aware of what is not covered.
- Fly you home for a relative's funeral (although you are maximum three days drive away)

It is important to check the small print to see if your insurance is invalidated by any activities, such as consuming alcohol. Generally travel cover is not provided in countries designated a War Zone or 'unsafe'. Check the Foreign Office web site for details of countries that British Citizens are advised not to travel to. There are many high street companies that provide travel insurance, but we recommend you visit either STA Travel www.statravel.co.uk Tel:08701 630026 or Endsleigh www.endsleigh.co.uk Tel: 0800 0283571, who offer comprehensive travel insurance, which should be suitable. Be aware that these policies may be voided if you return to the United Kingdom for more than 24 hours. So if you are planning to return only book insurance to that point, it can always be extended if plans change.

The Foreign Office

Everybody travelling abroad should contact the Foreign and Commonwealth Office to check their advice on countries. Travelling to countries identified as not recommended may put you at risk and may invalidate travel insurance, check with your provider. In addition the Foreign and Commonwealth Office provide information on insurance and health issues for travellers. Visit www.fco.gov.uk or contact the Foreign and Commonwealth Office on 0845 8502829. Those touring should aim to view this website regularly to ensure they don't suffer a surprising situation if local conditions change suddenly.

Medical

Your personal insurance will hopefully cover you in a medical emergency, however it's worth considering a few other factors;

European Health Insurance Card

Formerly the E111, this card covers medical care at state hospitals within the EU - check the form for participating countries. These forms are available free from the Post Office, Tel: 0845 6062030 or visit www.dh.gov.uk/travellers. This replaces and invalidates all previous E111 forms.

Vaccinations

There are several vaccinations required for some European destinations. Contact Masta on www.masta.org for a health brief of up to ten countries, costing £3.49, alternatively visit www.travelhealth.co.uk. Some vaccinations require several injections over a month and may have to be ordered, so contact your doctor in advance.

Prescriptions and over the counter medication

Ensure that you travel with your necessary prescription drugs as required and keep prescription details of any drugs you need. Medication can be expensive in Europe, particularly in Germany and Italy. Some medication is cheaper in Greece, Spain and Andorra where a prescription is unlikely to be needed. So top up your cabinet.

Medical kits

Medical Kits are available from chemists including Boots, which provide sterile needles etc, to be used in an emergency. It may be worth considering if you intend to travel to more deprived or isolated areas. Visit www.travelhealth.co.uk for various articles, health tips and an option to purchase items online.

Becoming ill

If you suffer from a medical problem abroad consider www.nhsdirect.nhs.uk for health advice. Alternatively visit the hospital or doctor, your campsite or tourist information should have this, alternatively follow hospital signs in town. Explaining problems can be difficult and you may have to wait for an English speaking doctor to be found. www.transmedi.com offers a service translating medical information about existing conditions. www.passthephone.com Tel: 0871 218200 offers a solution to this by providing a translation service at the end of a phone, advertised as 'from emergencies to booking a table at a restaurant'.

Other health issues

Mosquitoes: Unfortunately most of Europe is a mecca for mosquitoes and although these are unlikely to carry disease, always get medical advice based on the countries you intend to visit. The bites can be itchy and uncomfortable. Repellent, after bite and antihistamines should be packed. Finland appears to have the worst mozzies. If visiting Northern Scandinavia in Summer it is worth considering a mosquito head cover.

Water: The water in Italy and Spain can appear very dubious and a rich source of chlorine. Although it is excellent for removing tea stains, it may not be what you want to drink, possibly upsetting people with sensitive skin and stomachs. Consider having a water filter fitted or stick to bottled water. Always check it is drinking water - this should be clearly signed and often marked with the words 'eau potable'or 'trink wasser'.

Identification

Passports

You must have a valid passport to travel in Europe. Generally this needs to be valid for six months after your return. It is essential that this document is not lost so keep it in a secure place, preferably a safe.

Camping Card International (CCI)

This card is used instead of a passport when you book in at campsites It details your address and passport number. This ensures your passports remain in your possession, useful as some countries require you to carry your passport at all times (details are in the Caravan Club Europe guides). This card is accepted across Europe, some sites offer discount on production. The CCI accompanying book details country information on camping, free-parking and campsites that offer CCI discounts. For more information visit www.campingcardinternational.net. Swedish campsites don't accept CCI. Luckily they have their own which you must buy if you wish to use any site.

CCI cards are available from clubs affiliated to the AIT, FIA or FICC. The following organisations offer the CCI in the UK, although may only be available to members:

RAC www.rac.co.uk

The Caravan Club www.caravanclub.co.uk Tel: 01342 316101

The Camping and Caravanning Club www.campingandcaravanningclub.co.uk Tel: 02476 422024

The Motorcaravan Club www.motorcaravanners.org.uk Tel: 02088 933883

Have the following information when you phone: Date of Birth, Place of Birth, Nationality, Passport Number, Passport date of issue, Passport place of issue.

Driving licences

This document is of prime importance to any motorhome driver, it details vehicle restrictions and penalties. Always ensure you keep it in a secure place. On the continent most countries issue photo card licences. People with the old paper licences may need to show their passport as photo identification. Alternatively the licence can be returned to the DVLA and replaced with a European style photo licence. You must travel with both the plastic card and supporting paper copy.

Driving licence restrictions

If you passed your test before the 1 January 1997 you can drive a vehicle with a maximum weight of 7500kg and up to 8250kg if towing a trailer. Drivers over 70 are restricted to 3500kg, unless a medical is taken and submitted to the DVLA. If you have passed your test since 1 January 1997 you are limited to a maximum weight of 3500kg and limited to a maximum trailer weight of 750kg. To raise weight limit restriction on either licence further driving tests need to be taken. Visit the DVLA website or pick up a form from the Post Office.

The International Driving Permit

An additional driving permit may be required in some countries in Europe. As it costs very little it may be worth each driver purchasing one of these to be on the safe side, especially if you intend to drive out of the EU. They can be purchased from motoring organisations such as the AA or RAC.

Head Quarters (HQ)

Before you depart ask someone that you trust to manage your affairs, to receive your mail and be on the end of the phone if you need anything. Provide them with copies of all important documents which should be kept flat in a folder should they need to be faxed. No matter what goes wrong there is only one phone call needed to get assistance.

Document list kept by HQ and in motorhome safe

- A colour photocopy of passports and an original birth certificate (HQ) of each passenger. In the event of passports being lost these documents are required by the British Consulate.
- Copies of your European Medical Insurance Card and medical insurance so these can be activated on your behalf. Details of your blood group, vaccinations, any medical conditions and copies of any prescriptions.
- Copies of all documentation regarding the ownership of your vehicle, MOT's and insurance. Include a copy of relevant driving licences.
- Banking details so that money can be transferred to you if necessary. Ideally leave some money behind to cover any expenses and a little spare for contingencies.
- Leave a copy of next of kin details and phone numbers of anyone you may need to contact while you are away, for instance your alarm fitters/warranties/dealer.
- The Royal Mail will redirect post, at a cost, to a new address or a PO box. Contact the Royal Mail for details of these services.

- Consider leaving copies, or locations, of Wills and Power of Attorney documents.
- The original documents should be kept in a safe place in the motorhome.

Money

Bank accounts

Don't waste your weekly budget on bank charges every time you withdraw cash. Before leaving the UK find an account that allows you to withdraw your money without charge when using continental ATM machines and gives you a good rate of exchange. Accept nothing less than the commercial exchange rate, which compared to tourist rate will save a considerable amount over the months. Shop around as it is surprising what banks charge. Nationwide Building Society offers a 'Flex account' with a visa debit card that can be used all over Europe. They don't charge for any foreign transaction and give a commercial rate of exchange, internet banking included. It is excellent as you can keep your savings in a high interest account with no penalty instant access. It will be hard to find a better one, and probably saved us over £1000.

Cash and cash machines

ATM's, or cash machines, are widely available across Europe at service stations, banks and supermarkets. Most towns should have at least one, though rarely in villages or rural communities. Most cash machines offer a choice of languages so the transaction can take place in English. Bank ATM'S rarely charge for transactions Those in shops and garages often do, they do warn you so it's your choice.

For information on ATM cash machines accepting Visa or MasterCard visit www.visa.com or www.mastercard.com.

When entering non Euro countries cash can usually be withdrawn at the first town or fuel station, but don't panic as Euros will always be accepted near borders. Careful cash withdrawal management will avoid the use of bureau de change and double transactions for example changing Sterling into Euros into Lev. Placing sole responsibility of money outside the Euro zone to one person should avoid departing the country with money left over.

Euros are the principal currency even outside the Euro zone, replacing American dollars. If you intend to take travellers' cheques ensure they are in Euros again saving on double transactions. It is advisable to take a small amount of Euros when you depart the United Kingdom and keep a small amount of sterling for your return.

Credit cards

Credit cards are widely accepted and you must know your pin number. Withdrawing cash on your credit card will incur charges. Your credit card's monthly bill can be paid by direct debit from your bank account, or credit your card account before departure. We did the latter, finding that we only needed to use our Visa debit card.

Weekly budget

The cheapest budget for two people touring is around £250 per week. Restrained spending is required as this includes food, fuel, accommodation, repairs, tourism -literally everything except insurance. In Scandinavia this will be £300 as the cost of living and ferries stretch the budget. To stay within these figures you won't be able to eat out often, go to every tourist site or stay in campsites every night. If you stay on one site for an extended period you can expect to spend less. Many cater for long term visitors with free entertainment or cheap trips, not to mention the company and social life, which can build up. Based on this two people can look to spend £150-£200 per week, i.e. around £750 per month.

Staying in budget

For most of us everything comes down to economics. You must decide: how long you wish to go away; how much money you have; and where you wish to go; and how you wish to do it.

The longer you are away the easier it is to budget. Nevertheless you must log your expenses as they can easily run away from you. Purchase a simple cashbook available in most stationary departments. Start the week and write down everything you spend in the following columns: date, item, and cost. Add it up at the end of every week. This way the budget can be monitored and you can work out exactly where you are overspending, or if you are really lucky, under spending.

It is far cheaper to sit still on a campsite out of season than to tour, it is cheaper still using camper-stops and free-parking rather than campsites.

Tourism - Think carefully about the sights you wish to visit. There are many free sights, which are simply lesser known than their counterparts. You can gain a good idea of a sight by wandering around the outside before deciding whether to go in. Architecture and churches can provide some fantastic free days out. City cards can provide excellent value for money but you have to make the most of them and that means early starts and long days. Park outside big towns and cities for free and use public transport to get in. Grab a picnic from a supermarket or walk down back streets to have a cheaper lunch (surprisingly Chinese food is often the best value for money). Buy your tourist books in the UK as they are two if not three times more expensive abroad. Major tourist sites in Greece are free in the winter to EU citizens on Sundays.

Our diary entry for Florence reads: We didn't pay to go into anything so it meant we could wander around and enjoy the atmosphere. We figured we would return when there were less queues. But there was plenty of outdoor art and sculptures as well as churches to marvel at.

Motorhome size - Unfortunately in a lot of instances it does come down to size. Motorhomes over 6 metres are considered large and often pay more for pitches, tolls and ferries, twin axle and trailers attract additional cost. In several European countries motorhomes over 3.5 tons pay higher tolls, Austria being a prime example, failing to pay the correct fee can result in a large fine.

Fuel - Diesel is significantly cheaper on the continent than petrol. In France and Spain it is worth hunting out a Supermarket. These are clearly signed and fuel can be up to 15 cents a litre cheaper, also check for additional discount when shopping at the store.

When approaching borders look at the number plates of cars in the petrol stations and supermarkets, this indicates which country has cheaper fuel or food. In Southern Italy you have to be particularly vigilant as often the price advertised is only for the pump marked Fia Dante, the others are up to 10 cents per litre more. Fuel also tends to be cheap in principalities, such as Andorra.

Visit www.theaa.com/allaboutcars or Ceefax to get an idea of prices before you travel.

Although LPG is cheap on the continent it is not widely available in Spain, Germany, Greece or Scandinavia.

Receiving Post

If you need to receive post, such as green cards, insurance documents and bank cards try to have mail sent direct to a campsite, or Poste Restante to a post office of your choice. The document needs to be addressed:

Poste Restante
Surname, First name
Post Code
Town
Country

The Caravan Club Europe guides detail various postcodes for using this system. Poste Restante needs to be substituted for Post Lagernd in Germany and Austria, Fermo Posta in Italy and Lista de Correos in Spain. Letters and parcels are filed under the first letter of the first word, which may be your surname, first name, title or any other possibility making them difficult to track down. A passport is required to collect letters and some post offices may charge on collection. Items will only be held for one month. Motorhomers have reported varying success with this system, from super efficient to absolutely hopeless.

Www.thewrinklies.co.uk reads: ...we drove into Gibraltar again to collect our two mail items, one of which was replacement bankcards. Imagine our consternation when we were told that NEITHER the CD which Nicky posted 4 weeks ago, nor the package with the bank cards which had been sent registered 8 days before, had arrived. It would be stretching coincidence too far to think that the postal service could lose two letters addressed to me in the space of one month, so the only conclusion is that they are swilling around in Gibraltar's postal system. We know from a resident that there is a large delay in sorting mail because of a labour dispute...

Communication by phone and email

Phone

You can rely solely on pay phones but these often require cards. If you change countries regularly this may result in half used cards. When stopping in one country - payphones will be the cheapest option.

Mobile phones need to be enabled for European roaming. To ensure your phone works contact your provider and enquire about coverage. Prices vary widely and any call you receive from the UK will incur a roaming charge. The caller pays the standard UK charge and you make up the difference, so any call can be expensive. Text messages cost around 40p and are a cheap way to communicate. We used text messages to liaise a time we would phone friends and family from a phone box.

SIM4travel claims it charges significantly less for foreign mobile calls, with no charges for receiving calls in 61 countries, though text message costs stay the same. The initial SIM costs £29.95 with €5 of credit, top ups by phone or online cost €30, €50, €80 and €120 denominations. Their website details possible savings in individual countries. Contact the company by visiting their website www.SIM4travel.com as their phone line Tel: 0905 335 0336 charges 40p per minute.

Email and internet

Sending emails is the cheapest way to communicate and can be accessed freely across Europe. Tourist information offices and libraries normally provide free access. Internet cafes and campsites charge between €1 to €5 per hour. Many companies such as virgin and yahoo, provide free email addresses which can be set up in advance. Hotmail has so many graphics that many computers simply cannot open your messages.

Skype - is an Internet based telephone service that is accessible in many Internet café's across Europe. This is an easy, cheap and viable service that should prove useful to all travellers. There are small annual subscription charges for membership and voicemail. Calls between Skype numbers are free and calls to landlines are about 1.1 pence per minute. Live webcam calls are also free and video messages can be sent. There are many possibilities and we are going to subscribe. Visit www.skype.com

Laptop users - can purchase slot in data cards that work on the mobile phone networks allowing access to the internet. These charge per megabyte downloaded, this can be prohibitively expensive to use. Wireless LAN cards could provide free internet access. You need to find an area giving a signal (hotspot) - the lap top can then connect to the internet. In reality this is impractical as the system is designed to service a building and tracking down this type of hotspot is virtually impossible. Some campsites provide this service. BT open zone is a pay wireless internet access provider. They are part of the WBA wireless broadband alliance with partners around the world. Charges are per minute connected and are as varied as mobile phone tariffs. At the time of writing there were over 30,000 hotspots around the world and this figure is rising quickly. All the information required is on the website www.btopenzone.com This appears to be a viable option, mainly because you can quickly open and save internet pages you have previously found whilst using free tourist information and library terminals, you can also write emails in advance then paste them into the email page. Broadband can be accessed through a satellite dish but needs a mobile phone/modem for connection see www.avcbroadband.com. Inmarsat's Regional BGAN utilises a satellite modem the same size as a laptop that you roughly point in the direction of the satellite. Because the satellite footprint is so large there aren't the same problems as with satellite TV. This is only viable to serious users as the costs are high see www.action-replay.co.uk www.satelliteforcaravans.co.uk discusses using the internet with a laptop and mobile phone. As this is fast moving technology we will keep it updated on our website www.go-motorhoming.co.uk

2 Way radios

These can be purchased from around £20, and are useful for keeping in contact around the campsite, in the shops and whilst reversing (cheaper than a rear view camera). Two way radios and CB's are also a good way of keeping in touch if travelling in convoy, without the mobile phone costs. Remember that CB's require licences in the UK and if you intend to use them abroad check whether additional licences or laws need to be complied with.

Languages

There are two main tourist languages spoken across Europe, English and German. Germans dominate the European motorhoming community, so many camp sites speak German as opposed to English.

The Dutch are also motorhoming mad and are very useful as they generally speak both English and German, as do the Swiss. The Italians are a keen motorhoming nation and will speak to you whether or not they speak English or you speak Italian.

If you intend to travel predominantly in one country then learning that language would be useful. If you can't attend a language course then language tapes may provide the answer and are excellent entertainment whilst driving. In any country it is worth learning the basics of 'hello', 'goodbye', 'please', 'thank you', and 'I would like…'. Many guidebooks provide these basic words though a language dictionary is worth considering.

Travelling with pets

Pet passports make it possible to take your pet with you. Motorhomers take a variety of animals including dogs, cats, parrots and rabbits. Taking an animal brings both joy and added responsibility. There are important administration tasks that need to be completed, taking up to six months.

Visit the following websites for more information:

www.defra.gov.uk/animalh/quarantine/pets

www.petplanet.co.uk/petplanet/travel

www.drive-alive.co.uk/pet-travel.htm

The Camping and Caravanning Club offer pet insurance and can arrange your pet passport for you call Tel: 0870 201 2501 or www.dogsaway.co.uk

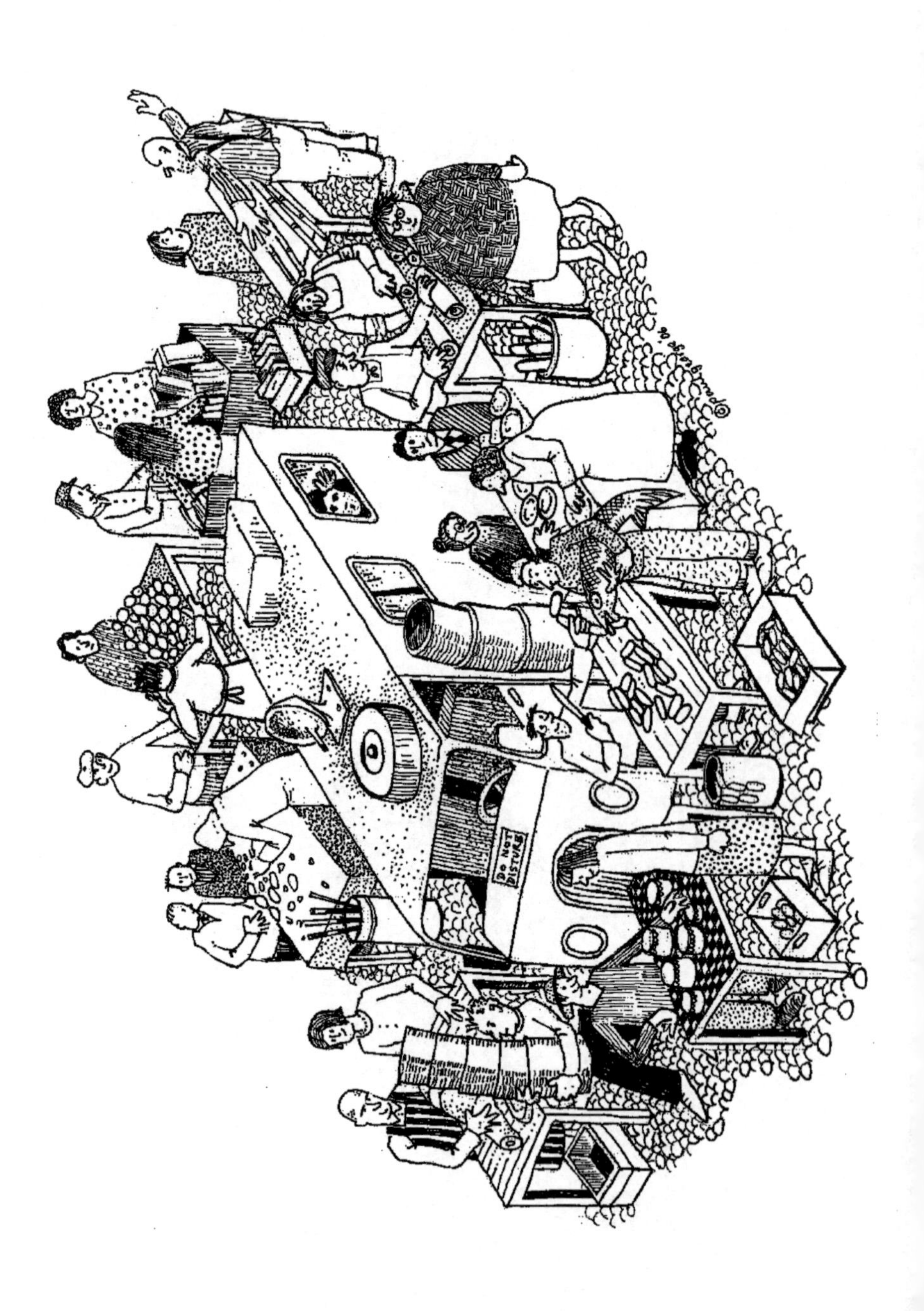
DO NOT DISTURB

In a motorhome you are at home wherever you are

You can cope in any motorhome but it will change your trip

Some owners of large motorhomes opt to tow a car

Ensure your motorhome can go where you want

One of the most popular free-parks in Spain

A farm style camper-stop in Denmark

Camper Dump

International free-park on a Sicillian beach

Campsite, camper-stop or free-park?

There may not be an inch of spare tarmac on mountain roads

Sometimes you may find the road has been completely removed

Driving in the rain can prove treacherous in Sicily

Waiting for a ferry in Norway

The weekly wash on a Swedish campsite

A very lucky couple permanently sited on a Greek campsite

Queuing for water with the locals in Bulgaria

Free-parking at the bottom of a ski lift at Bansko in Bulgaria

Broken down -21°C in Bulgaria

Romanian mountain roads in a blizzard, don't forget your snow chains

Chapter 6 - Accommodation; from Campsites to Free-parks

There are plenty of places to stay in Europe suiting every desire and budget. Whether you want luxurious campsites or to flex your wild side this chapter tells you how.

Campsites

There are around 30,000 across Europe which means you can stay at a different one every night for the next 82 years, most are open Easter to August. On the continent locals pitch for the season setting up in March with huge twin wheeled caravans, and awnings (containing fridge freezer, kettle, oven, TV, lounge furniture), white picket fence, lawn mower, and street lights. Sites are often very large, facilities may not be clean and they can be very expensive. There is no guarantee that the expensive campsites are better than the cheap ones, they vary widely.

Costs

Expect to spend at around £15 per night at campsites across Europe, more for capital cities, peak season and popular tourist destinations. Expect to pay for electricity, priced in a 3 amp, 6 amp and 16 amp scale, and you can even be charged for showers, hot water and have to provide your own toilet paper! It is worth investigating a site before agreeing to stay. This is common practice in Europe and no-one will be offended.

Long stays are cheaper than short, out of season cheaper than peak and discounts are available from campsite chains and various schemes. For long stays it is possible to get half price discounts using Alan Rogers Camping Cheques i.e. 60 nights for 30 cheques. The accompanying guidebook details many offers available on a variety of sites and includes a naturist section. The Camping Card ACSI offers the cheapest stays and requires the least outlay, ideal when on a tight budget or unsure how often campsites will be required. Some campsites using this or the camping cheque scheme also offer 7 nights for 6 cheques and 14 nights for 12 cheques, other sites offer 10 per cent when a CCI card is used

Discounts - Various discounts are available. There are a range of out of season discount schemes based on two people per night either motorhome or caravan, including electricity.

Alan Rogers Camping Cheques cost £10.30 per night, and are valid for two years. There are 555 participating campsites in 20 countries offering low season accommodation. Some campsites offer 7 nights for 4 cheques or 60 nights for 30 cheques, always ask as sometimes it is cheaper to pay cash. These cheques need to be purchased in advance. Tel: 0870 4054057
www.campingcheque.co.uk

Touring Cheque, £10.25 per night, with 119 campsites, only 35 of these outside of France. Both camping Cheque and Touring Cheque have increased in price significantly over the last few years making them a considerable outlay. There is no cash refund so you have to use all the cheques. Tel:0870 9060123
www.touringcheque.co.uk

The Camping and Caravanning Club sell Freedom Camping vouchers for £7.50 each in a book of 30, these obtain discounts at 95 sites through 13 countries listed in their Carefree brochure. Tel: 02476 422024 www.campingandcaravanclub.co.uk

A new contender on the scene is the camping card ACSI. This system involves purchasing a discount card and book for £6, although you then have to send a text to register the card and the return text costs £1.50. If you show the card at sites listed in the book you are entitled to stay at a discount price listed in the book, either €13.50, €11.50, or €9.50 per night for two adults including electricity. This scheme has 667 participating campsites including 290 in France, 89 in the Netherlands and 88 in Italy. This scheme offers the biggest discount and the widest choice of campsites with very little outlay. Visit www.camping-card.com for more details.

Hidden costs - Many campsites itemise their bills, for example: motorhome (small, medium and large), caravan, car, trailer, scooter, person, children, pets, electricity, awning, hot water, showers, swimming pool, security pass (deposit). These costs add up and can make what appears to be a cheap site expensive.

Booking

There is no need to book in advance except in high season; the last week in July until the third week in August and July in Scandinavia when Europe goes on holiday. Even then some sites retain touring pitches or squeeze you in somewhere. It is common practice in Europe to turn up, look around and if you like what you see book in. No one will be offended either way and apart from being quite liberating can lead to an enjoyable holiday where you get exactly what you want. If you are worried you won't get a pitch due to bank holidays, you can always phone the site and confirm a pitch and sit out the bank holiday for a few days - all campsite books have phone numbers of listed campsites.

Normally pitches have to be vacated by 10am and booking in from 2pm. Late departure or early arrival can incur additional costs.

CCI (Camping Card International) cards are advisable, they're used instead of passports to book in at campsites, some offer discounts on production. Do check that the CCI returned is yours. See ***Chapter 5*** for more information.

There is a chance, in spite of careful planning, you arrive at a site you intend to stay on and after a day, week, month or even longer, you hate it. Don't stay for the sake of it, this is your holiday and you should enjoy it. There are hundreds of sites open in the winter so there is always somewhere else to go. Speak to other campers, consult the Caravan Club European guide or search the internet.

Our diary states: Then onto Florence. We were trying to find a camper-stop in our German book. We drove round and round for hours in the heat before giving up and following the campsite signs. The first was about 8km out of town with fantastic views of Florence [but after wandering around] decided it was too expensive. The second was in the youth hostel grounds and a little noisy. The third was the other side of town but so close you could see the dome – it was stunning at night. The only problem was it was on a hill and impossible to get level [it also cost €27 per night!].

We frequently turned up at campsites, and after wandering around decided not to book in. At popular tourist spots we would always visit more than one campsite. We never find it necessary to book in advance, but we always try to travel out of season.

Problems

Access - Trees can be a big problem on Mediterranean sites, they are planted to provide shade in the main summer season. Often they make getting around the site difficult for high or long vehicles. Most campsites are planted with deciduous trees. In the warmest areas these hang on to their leaves until December. Out of season it can be difficult to get out of the shade, which can make the days cold and the evenings draw in quickly.

Levels - It is unlikely that you'll experience many level nights, many campsites don't consider it important and at camper-stops and free-parks you accept what is available. A simple small two-way spirit level will give you an idea as you jiggle around on the chosen spot. After a while an unlevelled motorhome becomes tolerated. Always think about where you sleep in the motorhome and aim to position the motorhome so you sleep feet down, and head up, in bed. If you intend to use predominantly campsites then consider taking three or even four chocks. Invest in a chopping board with a drip edge to avoid spills when preparing food.

Marking your pitch - Simply leaving a table and chairs out is enough. Some use small signs but this is something else to store and carry.

Campsite showers - Shower cubicles often have only one or no hook so a bathrobe or dressing gown that can be thrown over the door with a pocket for keys is useful. Not all are that clean so it is worth considering taking some shower shoes, simply waterproof shoes you wear when showering so you don't have to come in contact with the floor. Be warned cheap flip-flops fling mud and dust up your damp legs.

Rules - Some campsites insist that swimming trunks as opposed to shorts are worn in the pool, mainly in France, while others insist on swimmers wearing hats. Both can be expensive on the campsite so consider purchasing these in advance. Charcoal barbeques are predominantly not allowed on continental campsites. Some also prohibit air conditioners and most ban generators.

Etiquette

There are certain rules that need to be followed to ensure you get on with your fellow campers. Always wipe up and remove any food when using the washing up sinks. When using the showers mop up any water residue, soap and powder.

When moving around the campsite do not pitch invade, it might be the quickest way to the shower block but people do not appreciate you cutting through the pitch they are paying for. Be aware of your noise, you may like the tune on the radio but your neighbours might not.

Setting up

Park near the entrance, though not obstructing it and enter reception to enquire about price. Walk the site, inspecting pitches and facilities before informing reception if you will stay. To choose the correct pitch, think about satellite reception, hours of sunlight, noise, distance to facilities and gradient of pitch. Return to reception and confirm pitch location. Fill up with water and empty tanks if necessary then set up on your pitch, level camper, plug in electricity checking polarity, turn on gas, and switch fridge over from 12v to either gas or mains electricity. Relax! Then think of something to do.

Small campsites (mini camping)

There are plenty of small, CL or farm style campsites across Europe, widely known as 'mini camping', for a quieter, less commercialised experience. Prices vary from €5 to €10 per night, being similar to certified locations found in the UK. These can be harder to find but tourist information can point you in the right direction.

In Holland there are plenty of these and books are available at Tourist Information. In Italy look for Agro tourism signs whilst driving, leaflets at Tourist Information and bookshops. These sites are farms and vineyards looking for extra income and the possibility of selling their produce, these farm stops can be a fun, educational experience. Often smaller sites are visible or signed off

minor roads. As always it's about confidence and simply pulling in and enquiring. Details are available in ***Chapter 9: Country Guides*** and some are listed in Camper stop books and the Caravan Club Europe Guides.

In Eastern Europe some campsites only list facilities for tents, however motorhomers recently report that they have been able to use these tent only campsites.

Naturist

There is an extensive range of naturist campsites large and small across Europe these are often in fantastic locations and can offer a relaxing, if not different holiday. Don't feel you are making a life style choice that you must stick to, it is possible to be a 'holiday naturist'. The continentals are a lot more relaxed about naturism and it is possible to book into a site without showing any identification, i.e. a British Naturist ID card, although some sites do prefer it or require passport photos for identification cards. Smaller naturist sites offer a rally like feel with communal meals and group activities.

Naturism has few simple rules - you don't have to be naked all the time, sometimes it's too cold, you're sun burnt or you are leaving the site. Most times nudism is only compulsory around the pool. You do have to be respectful of other people, no laughing, pointing or photos (unless you ask first for the latter). The Caravan Clubs Europe guide lists naturist sites, as does Alan Rogers Camping Cheque guide or contact British Naturism on www.british-naturism.org.uk for more details.

Campsite Guide books

There are plenty of campsite guides, here are just a few:

The Caravan Club Europe Vol. 1 & 2, updated annually available from the Caravan Club. On the surface these are simply guides to campsites but also includes an incredibly useful information section. Campsite reports are written and updated by members. A good variety of campsites are listed from CL style to large commercial. Information includes price, directions, opening dates and facilities as well as the year the site was reviewed. There is a map showing the location of the campsites identifying which are open all year. It is worth remembering that these books err on the site of caution, urging against free-parking. But don't be put off as the information provided and site reviews are invaluable, allowing you to always find a campsite when you need one.

They also include guides to each country, including public holidays/shop opening times, motoring regulations, fuel availability, speed limits, international road signs, motorway tolls, emergency numbers, legal and insurance requirements, pet advice, accident and emergency procedures and medical advice, customs regulations and documents, British and Irish embassies/consulates.

We recommend you take the most recent copies of these guides.

Le Guide Official Camping and Caravanning, covers 10,800 sites in France available from the Camping and Caravanning Club

Guia Camping, covers sites in Spain and Portugal available from the Camping and Caravan Club

ADAC, the German automobile association produce camping books. *Camping Caravanning Fuhrer* divided into two volumes either Deutschland and Nordeurope or Sudeurope. These books are written in German. Visit www.adac.de/campingfuhrer or buy from bookshops in Germany or www.amazon.de

Alan Rogers, www.alanrogers.com Tel: 0870 405 4055 also produce a variety of campsite guides including *Europe, France, Italy, Spain & Portugal, Central Europe and Britain & Ireland.*

Camper-stops

There is one exclusive advantage of taking a motorhome to Europe, they allow you to use camper-stops, rest stops dedicated for motorhomes, except in Italy where caravans may stay too. These stops range from designated areas in car parks, which normally have dumping, and water facilities, to locations that campsites can't rival. They are identifiable by the international motorhome sign and are detailed in various publications available in each country. They provide an excellent opportunity to meet other motorhomers but you do need to be self-contained as toilets or showers may not be nearby. Although they don't sound very glamorous or appealing they are often in amazing places with no nearby campsite.

These range from free to €5 per night and offer excellent value for money. There are plenty of camper-stop guides that will soon earn back their initial cost. Probably the most appealing fact is there are enough of them that are free that it would be possible to never pay for camping. Look for those described as gratuite (France), gratuita (Italy) or kostenlos (Germany). In reality those that do charge are only a few euros and give access to major tourist sites or towns as well as farm and guesthouse sites. They are an excellent stop off point for lunch and essential for those on a budget.

In this publication they are referred to as camper-stops but in every country they have a different name. The British campaign for their introduction refers to them as Stop-overs, France call them Aires, in Germany they're called Stellplatz, Italy Aree di Sosta, and Norway they are referred to as Bobils. Surprisingly only a few exist in Spain, primarily in the north.

Types of camper-stop

Camper-stops have four main forms:

- First there are sani stations. These are areas where motorhomes can dump waste, refill with water and sometimes charge batteries but cannot stay overnight. These can be located in garages or car parks and are either a tap and grate system or the facilities are contained in a box. Generally they all look the same and it doesn't take long for a keen eye to spot them.

- Secondly there are community stops, normally free. These are often car parks where the community has allotted space to encourage motorhomers to visit, these often have dumps and taps. Some in France have free electricity, ideal for Winter and Spring touring. These are the type we hunt out as they take you to undiscovered hamlets as well as city centres.

- Thirdly there are campsites where motorhomers who arrive after 4pm and leave before 10am pay a reduced fee. Some countries, predominately Scandinavia, promote this system and it is generally detailed in tourist information guides for those countries. There are sometimes restrictions on using the dumping facilities. Be sure when booking in that everybody is clear that you are using the 'camper stop' the name used in every country.
- Fourthly there are vineyards, farms and people's gardens. Not all have facilities but offer a CL style of camping. These are available in Denmark, Germany, Italy, France and Romania. These sites are found throughout the main camper-stop books (see individual countries for details). In France there is also the French Passion scheme available only to self sufficient motorhomes - bring your own water and don't expect to be able to dump - for a fee of €27 per annum you can stay on a variety of farms and vineyards for free.

Camper-stops are ideal for a number of reasons: they can be used to visit larger towns as many are in the suburbs near railway stations saving the expense of inflated campsite fees. They provide a recognised place to stop when you only want to have lunch or make a short visit to town. They are clearly detailed in several books, although in foreign languages these are generally easy to follow and often less hassle than trying to find a free-park.

> Www.thewrinklies.co.uk wrote: Our first experience of legal & free camping. Only information we have on these facilities is a French book, which means it's a bit hit and miss!
>
> We came upon this one by seeing the sign. It had no facilities and was situated on a piece of wooded land with a restaurant at the road edge. We parked behind the restaurant, felt more secure there!! In the morning we laughed at our nervousnes.

TIR parks

Those travelling to countries in the former Eastern Bloc, will find most campsites closed outside the main Summer season. free-parking is illegal, however it is our experience away from the main routes where there is no other option, you are left to your devices. Those wishing to visit these countries outside of these periods may need to use TIR parking areas. Details of TIR parking is available on www.iru.org/publications/welcome.E.html go to 'the bookshop' and then 'truck parking areas in Europe' to download a PDF.

> Our diary reads: Its minus 15, we're in a windswept TIR park in Romania in a blizzard and I'm so happy! We can't stay at the campsite [its closed] and we cant free-park – its too difficult in these temperatures. So we follow signs to a TIR park. Its run by an old man who is so friendly – we parked the motorhome out of the wind and we even have electric. We spend the evening in front of the wood fire in his cabin drinking brandy, talking in mime.

Further Information

www.eurocampingcar.com/uk is a site used by motorhomers across Europe and has some interesting facilities and links, a map gives an idea of where camper-stops are located but in reality it is worth purchasing the official publications.

Camper-stop guide books

Europe Guides

CamperStop Europe, This camper-stop guide details 6200 camper-stops across Europe. It is a multi language booklet and is the only camper-stop guide we know that contains information in English. *Available from Vicarious Books at www.go-motorhoming.co.uk Tel: 0131 208 3333*

The Official Guide Motorcaravan Tourist Stop Overs, this covers 6085 camper stops focussing on France. Available from the Camping and Caravan Club, this French guide covers camper stops in Germany and Italy plus a spattering of other countries.

Reise Mobil Bord Atlas lists camper stops mainly in Germany but also covers Italy and France in detail, plus Belgium, the Netherlands and some other countries. As this is the German guide it is written in German, however we have found this one of the easiest guides to use.

Country Specific

Le Guide National des Aires de Services camping-cars details 1350 Aires in France. This guide is available from the hypermarkets in France.

La Super Carte by Camping Car Magazine is a fold out map detailing 2850 Aires de Service. It is not as good as the books but should be enough to get by with.

France Passion; where invitations, valid for a year from Easter, are purchased to stay overnight on participating farms and vineyards throughout France.www.france-passion.com

ADAC publication *Stellplatz Deutschland* details German Camper-stops, available from bookshops across Germany.

Plein Air Portolano Per Camper E Caravan this details camper stop facilities in Italy, with some in France and Germany. www.pleinair.it

The Camper Guide Danmark produced by DACF details sani stations, farms, Camper-stop campsites and community spots through out Denmark. This book can be difficult to find in the country itself, but if you hunt hard enough you may find one. Alternatively visit www.dacf.dk before you depart.

Free-parking

This has a few names including 'free camping' and 'wild camping' however free-parking describes it better, as that is essentially what you are doing. Free refers to both the freedom from campsite constraints, and the price. Parking by the side of the road is legally allowed in some European countries and can sometimes, especially in Scandinavia, be your only option. The German motorhomers excel at free-parking, so if you are struggling for guidance follow their lead, they are always happy to help and a big percentage speak good English. Always free-park as considerately as possible, trying to cause the least offence to locals. Remember this is a luxury or a necessity, and should never be considered a right.

Reality

You can stay in some fantastic locations but you won't find an idyllic beach every night, car parks and lay-bys will provide 90 per cent of night stops. Free/wild camping is misleading as they suggest that you unpack and set up as if on a site. Mostly when free-parking the object is to remain inconspicuous and available to leave at a moment's notice, so unpacking is unrealistic. In countries where stopping by the side of the road is legal, camping by the side of the road is not. This means that items should not be placed around the motorhome, such as tables, chairs and bikes and if towing a caravan it should remain hitched to the car.

Location

Finding a night stop better than a car park, or camper-stop, can be exhausting. The best way to locate them is to ask other motorhomers. Always take your map and write the locations down on the map. Some free-parks are busy while others are isolated spots, there is a good network between motorhomers and information changes annually. Scandinavia offers endless idyllic free-park possibilities, but the Mediterranean coast has few. Those with idealistic dreams of Spain will be disappointed, as this is the hardest country in which to free-park, mainly due to its popularity. The Camping Card International book contains a brief outline for many European countries of the legalities of free-parking. Country specific information is provided in the *country guides* in ***Chapter 9***.

Being moved on

Being moved on means being asked to leave by an official, often the police. If you are 'knocked up' a common response is that you are resting or that you are only staying overnight, don't assume that because its legal you won't be disturbed but if you are it's normally a brief chat with an official and at the very worst you are asked to leave. These are examples of notices handed to us in Spain; 'You are camping on a forbidden place it is not allowed.

Please go to an admitted camping place or ask for the nearly tourist office.' The other read 'Phohibid to park caravans and vans in the main area of Peniscola'.

There are ways of parking to ensure you won't get disturbed; don't park where it clearly signs not to, don't block drive ways or entrances, avoid the touristy areas where they are likely to encounter many motorhomes. Don't expect the locals to be delighted when you block their view with your motorhome, try to imagine how you would feel if a motorhome turned up outside your house? Remember, if you think it's a good free-park, the locals may regard it as a good liaison spot, so you spend the night with the town's lovers. Motorhomers seem to be uncontrollably drawn to the coast, so in popular areas it may be advisable to head slightly inland.

Golden rules and safety

There are simple procedures that most motorhomers follow when free-parking. Stop in an illuminated area close to habitation, so you can raise the alarm if necessary. Small town squares normally have parking places and are a good place to stop. Always park so you can drive off at a moment's notice, face your exit, put everything away before you go to bed, do not put on external silver screens, internal ones are fine. Allow time to investigate your free-park, stop for a cup of tea or a meal and watch what and who is about. Have a walk around the area and familiarise yourself with it and have a drink in the nearest bar so locals are not suspicious of you. If possible park with other motorhomers and try to talk to your neighbours so they know who should be entering your motorhome. Avoid parking in motorway service stations including main routes, pull off and find a quieter town or village. Talk to other motorhomers as they will let you know what is going on but take it with a pinch of salt as all the bad stuff always appears to happen to someone else. Once you've done all that, relax and enjoy the biggest freedom that motorhoming gives you - the ability to be at home wherever you are.

We free-parked throughout Europe, and thanks to other motorhomers of all nationalities, we stayed in some truly amazing locations, integrated into communities and had experiences we could not have in campsites. We only encountered problems in Spain being knocked up three times, once a note was put on the windscreen asking us to leave. Whilst on a deserted mountainside lay-by in the middle of the night, police woke us, they asked how long we were staying but they let us stay the night. In a small port we were asked to leave by being given a multi-lingual leaflet. None of these experiences were ever threatening. Many motorhomers when asked if they free-park respond that they feel much safer in a campsite, we believe this is a false sense of security, as crime does happen on campsites. Thankfully we encountered no crime in campsites, camper-stops or free-parks. Maybe it's because we're British, a minority motorhoming nation, but we were treated with great respect and often unprecedented acts of kindness. People fundamentally are good and we were often helped out whether we needed it or not. When free-parking in towns, check to see if the market is held there. We were woken early several times. Still, you don't have far to carry your shopping.

Everyday essentials

Wherever you choose to stay the daily chores still have to be done. This section explains how to get the necessities done while on tour or on site.

Laundry

Whilst launderettes are available on the continent, they can be difficult to find and expensive. Most campsites have some sort of laundry system, from service washing to hand washing sinks which are good, especially if they have free hot water. Campsite washing machines are easy, but not necessarily cheap.

Drying - is easy in warm climates, simply line drying either on your pitch or using the site washing lines, although it is best to buy sheets and clothing that dry quickly. In Summer there is no need to take two sets of bedding, just wash on a good drying day.

On inclement days it is possible to string the washing through the motorhome and dry whilst you driving. Alternatively a motorhome bathroom can be used as a drying room: open the top vent, use clothes hangers, open the bathroom door, and aim a fan heater in - ideal when on a campsite where you have paid for electricity. A carousel is ideal for smalls and swimming costumes, and can be suspended from cycle rack or handle outside whilst free-parking. Some campsites provide clothes spinners free of charge, significantly reducing drying times.

Washing Machines - If you intend to spend the majority of your time on a campsite with electricity you may wish to buy a mini electric machine. These are available from www.towsure.co.uk and other camping shops, as are hand turned washing machines. One brand called a Wonder Wash, pressure is created when hot water is added and manually turned, actually wash the clothes and bedding well. It may be less convenient than an electric washing machine but it is fun, cost effective and can be used anywhere you have access to water. The manual washing machine is also considerably lighter than an electric equivalent.

Www.thewrinklies.co.uk write: 'We have a manual washing machine, looks a bit like R2D2 with one arm! but it does a creditable job of washing clothes. Actually it's the second one we have had, we bought the first one in Norway after working out we had spent £15 that week on washing. ...but it was becoming a little tired and rickety (quiet in the cheap seats!) so we bought a new one last week.'

Shopping

Shopping is surprisingly easy. There are hypermarkets across Europe and most don't have height restrictions, so it is possible to stock up at cheap prices. Continental signing laws allow hypermarkets to sign from a great distance. As in the United Kingdom hypermarkets vary in price, some offer discounts on fuel when you shop in store, so investigate this before you fuel up. Large campsites have shops on site, though convenient they can be expensive, smaller sites may sell fresh daily bread - possibly ordered by putting your name on a list. Buying long life products instead of fresh, for example UHT milk, reduces the need to shop regularly. Make the most of your fridge by removing bulky packaging. Freezers, no matter how small, are ideal for meat. For best use of space, repack meal size portions into freezer bags before freezing. This way at least a week's worth of meat can be kept, freeing up fridge space for other products. Crusty bread is a motorhome nightmare, the worst being the French baguette, which fires shards around the motorhome, fixing in upholstery, curtains and bedding. Hence many motorhomers opt to cut bread outside.

Food and drink in transit - Prevent messy spills by keeping items in the fridge in sealed containers, plastic take away containers are ideal. Ensure milk and other liquids have pop down or screw tops, rather than a tear off opening although a peg helps. Free up space by using bags instead of bulky packaging.

Loss of fridge pin: If your fridge pin gets lost or broken a golf tee is a good substitute. Always leave your fridge door ajar when not in use, to keep fresh.

Cloth bag - In many continental supermarkets, especially

Scandinavia they either don't have, or charge, for carrier bags. Fold up cloth bags are stronger than carrier bags, and more practical when walking or cycling with shopping. The National Trust sell a rucksack that folds into a bum bag priced at £12.99

Alcohol - Alcohol is prohibitively expensive in Scandinavia so it is advisable to take your own. In the rest of Europe cheap wine, around €1 per litre, can be bought in supermarkets. Cantine should be visited in Italy, where local wine can be purchased for the same price but you can try before you buy, look for shops that have lots of vats or barrels. Re-use is common across Europe, an example is bottled beer in Germany, which can be prohibitively expensive because of the bottle refund called 'pfant'. Check the refund policy, as own store returns may be necessary. Be warned that some German beer is 15 per cent alcohol - the same as wine, both in bottles and bars. It's a shame it's so strong as blond beer is very moreish.

Cooking

Curiously an area of contention: not because there is any argument, obviously the co pilot's job except for BBQ's which if you have followed our lead you will leave behind. In reality two gas rings are adequate for cooking an infinite variety of meals. We have three examples and two views; our touring motorhome only had three rings, which was right for that situation, our wintering caravan had an oven as well, which we used one and a half times a week, our current motorhome has an oven (which appears to have been un-used), hob and grill which together create more noise than a touring rock band on otherwise quiet country lanes. A tea towel under the hob cover helps a little with the noise. In our opinion an oven in a motorhome is an unnecessary waste of weight and space, however those wintering should take an electric mini oven/grill. Using cheap, lightweight pans are a false economy, unless washing up is your hobby. A large lidded non-stick pan is useful for cooking one-pot wonder meals. Some motorhomers use pressure cookers as they feel this saves on gas and reduces condensation if opened outside. See ***Chapter 4 Preparing your Motorhome*** for other cooking essentials.

Condensation will occur in cool climates when the humidity inside your motorhome exceeds 60 per cent. This can become a problem in poorly ventilated leisure vehicles leading to mildew growth. Cooking adds a big percentage of moisture into the equation, not only is steam produced but for every litre of LPG burnt one litre of water is released. Over cooker extractor fans should be used if fitted, at the very least roof vents should be opened when cooking. See Fiamma/Omni vent in ***Chapter 4 Add-ons and Extras*** for an excellent condensation control solution. Condensation is one of the reasons, as well as smell, why so many winterers cook in their awnings.

Rubbish

In most Mediterranean countries it is easy to discard rubbish in communal wheelie bins, usually the home of neighbourhood cats. Even in countries that do not use this system litterbins are available. Milk and fruit juice cartons and lidded jars work well for wet food such as fat, starchy water that could cause blockages and will make the waste tank smell. These containers can also be used for waste toilet tissues. Expect to produce one litre and one carrier bag worth of rubbish per day.

Tips and tricks

A universal plug: If you intend to use sinks in campsites, it is worth having a universal plug as plugs are very rarely available. Various types of universal plugs can be bought from camping shops and travel companies, so keep one in your wash bag.

Very long armed, thick rubber gloves: To be used when emptying the toilet, as sometimes there is slight spillage. Washing out the cassette can be a messy process especially if the toilet emptying facility is grotty. These gloves should be kept separate, those with a cassette toilet compartment could place the gloves there.

Stiff bristled plastic brush: Usually purchased as part of a dustpan and brush set. This can be used to brush out the motorhome instead of using a vacuum cleaner, brush off mud and snow from clothing and shoes, also used to wash the motorhome, and wash off boots and equipment.

Shoes outside: leave your welly shoes or clogs under the motorhome when parked up and use these when popping in and out of the motorhome. They rarely get wet and save on a considerable amount of cleaning. You will, at some stage, run over them normally seeing them in your rear view mirror, so they need to be cheap.

Doormat: This helps reduce dust and dirt entering the motorhome. An outside mat means shoes can be taken off and left outside while one just inside the door picks up any residue and can be shaken out easily.

Blanket cushions: By placing a small, possibly fleecy as very light, blanket in a cushion cover a useful cushion is gained as well as a cover for cool evenings or warm nights.

Make your own time: We find, especially in Greece during the winter, that setting your clocks forward an hour or two is very beneficial. Therefore you make the most of the daylight, also helping to getaway early and beat busy periods at tourist sites and booking in at campsites.

Travelogues

The following websites may be interesting for those wishing to get an idea about life on the road. These are personal websites of motorhomers detailing the daily obstacles and joys of life on the road:

www.thewrinklies.co.uk Laurie and Anne's site who kindly let us use their diary entries.

www.a-motorhome-on-tour.co.uk

www.xor.org.uk

www.magbaztravels.com

Chapter 7 - Life on the road

Where and when to go

There are endless possibilities and places to visit in Europe. Some people aim to go to the furthest compass points (guilty as charged), others don't plan at all (still guilty). Forward planning or pursuing interests, will provide structure to your tour, you simply can't see everything. Bad planning can lead to hundreds of unnecessary miles and visiting countries at the wrong time, experiencing temperatures too hot or cold, or missing sites of interest (been there, done that, and got the 'guilty' T-shirts). Wherever you choose to go we recommend that you only plan to do four-month trips.

Spring

Spring is a wonderful time to travel as the continent wakes up for a new season, with lovely weather and flowers, but beware as some places are still off limits. Scandinavia is still very cold with many roads closed due to snow. Those intending to visit Scandinavia, or travel through mountainous regions should be prepared with snow chains. Efforts should be made to ascertain if your chosen route is passable.

Southernmost Spain, Greece and Italy will be delightful and can be enjoyed before temperatures become unbearable. The sea will still be cold so don't expect to swim.

Summer

Europe can get extremely hot in the Summer, which may sound fantastic but Southern Spain, Italy, or Greece without (and sometimes with) air conditioning can be unbearable, not to mention the risk of dehydration and heat stroke. One motorhoming couple based in Greece found that even two air conditioners were not enough. At 35°C plus you may find your motorhome suffers as non-setting mastic seals could start to melt. Even in Central Europe it can be very hot and being high up in the mountains under a shady tree is your best option. Many Southern Europeans take August off and Scandinavians July so campsites can then be full to capacity and charging peak rates. With this in mind Northern Europe in August is an excellent place to go, France,

Belgium, Holland, Germany, and North Eastern Europe offering enjoyably warm temperatures.

If budgets allow, Norway is well worth a visit and provides temperatures more like a British Summer with the rain to match. If a wet summer is forecast, Scandinavia might be worth missing. Likewise if a heat wave is forecast you will be able to enjoy the beach delights of the Arctic Circle. Minor motorhome modifications may be needed, first against mosquitoes, which are prolific and secondly to ensure it can be fully blacked out as 24 hour daylight plays havoc with natural sleep patterns. People are often up and about in the middle of the night so avoid pitching near communal areas as these can be very noisy.

Bear in mind that the 'season' in Europe ends in the last week of August. After this campsites take on a ghost town appearance, but have the advantage of cheap rates in glorious September sunshine.

Heat management - Simple heat management techniques can help you enjoy the sunshine without having to use air conditioning. The biggest problem is leaving the motorhome unattended. Most insurance companies state that all windows and top vents must be closed. Temperatures rise quickly and heat both the fabric and contents of the motorhome, this heat is released like a storage heater at bed time. This is either good or bad depending on evening temperatures. The best night time cooling is achieved by having a Fiamma/Omni vent fan blowing cool air into the motorhome up to $35m^3$/minute, although an oscillating fan heater with the heater elements turned off is fine. A Fiamma/Omni vent fan combined with an all weather top vent cover/cowl means that the daytime heat build up can be continually extracted/vented even if you suspect rain. Running the blown air system can help in distributing cool air. Always try to park in the shade. If you are leaving the motorhome for several hours, consider where the sun will move. Ideally your motorhome will be fitted with window screens, these usually have a silver backing and should be shut when parked. Most heat will travel through the cab so curtains or blinds on these windows should also be shut. Heat reflective windscreen covers suitable for C-class motorhomes are available cheaply from automotive stores. Alternatively cover the windscreen outside using a tarpaulin or blanket. The fridge will struggle in really hot conditions this is why Saharan expedition vehicles are fitted with compressor fridges. To give your fridge the best chance always park with the fridge side away from the sun. A small 12v fan can be added to remove excess heat although this should be unnecessary if the fridge is fitted correctly. When camped up the awning provides excellent shade so use this to take the brunt of the sun. In really hot temperatures head north, ideally to a forested area and spend the hot weather under the trees.

Autumn

The continental season ends the last week in August and sites begin to dismantle and shut up. This may come as a surprise as the weather is still fine. By consistently heading south a temperature of 25°C can be maintained well into December. This is a fantastic harvest period when grapes, olives and citrus fruits are gathered, the beaches deserted and seas are warm. Some Eastern European countries require you to stay on campsites by law. Most campsites are completely shut by the end of September, so research will be needed if you intend to travel in this period. The Caravan Club Europe book shows, on a map, campsites open all year round, marked in red.

Winter

The time of year when an electric blanket/mattress cover is probably worth having in your inventory, whether heading for the slopes or the sand (we use one but don't tell anybody). To be brutally honest if you are long terming, once it's too cold to sit outside in central Europe you're best bet is to join the migration south.

Hot wintering (sun seeking)

The term sun seeker refers to motorhomers and caravanners who flock south for the winter, predominantly to Southern Spain, the warmest place in continental Europe. The primary period is January to March although people start heading south from October and may not return until May.

Winter weather - Wherever you go you cannot escape the rain so you will need to be prepared for wet days. If you are after sun

Spain is the warmest European country. Most days will be warm enough for shorts and sitting outside, even though the shade and the sea are cool. Don't expect Spain to be quiet, there will be plenty of British company and the coast caters well for long term winter visitors. For first time winterers Spain is the best destination and if you get itchy feet it is very convenient to visit Portugal or Morocco.

Morocco has increased in popularity over the last few years and in 2005/06 an alleged 1000 motorhome free-park took place in the Moroccan desert. Although this country has previously been viewed as a frontier in motorhoming it appears to be becoming more accessible, with the only reported problems being bureaucracy at the border. Local people service this temporary gathering, bringing fresh produce daily, removing waste and selling the obligatory rug all at reasonable prices. The best way to source information is to find motorhomes with camel and palm tree motifs (a sign of a visit to Morocco) or those returning with a rug on the roof!

Sicily provides some possibilities, a small free-parking community of less than one hundred motorhomes tour the island. The facilities here are very limited and you have to be prepared to be totally self-sufficient. It is colder than Spain, and we only found three good value campsites, the rest were expensive or grubby.

Greece is also colder than Spain being the furthest to travel, with additional ferry costs, but there are some good deals at the few campsites that remain open. Few make it to Greece and even less British visitors, so don't be surprised if you are on your own most of the time. You must be good with your own company and know how to entertain yourself. In all these places it will still rain and after Christmas be too cold to swim for most people. In the 2004/05 Winter, Spain experienced snow and freezing conditions.

Crowding - Southern Spain can get very busy; booking a pitch can be difficult at peak times especially if you have a large motorhome.

Crowding is not exclusive to Spanish campsites, the free-parking fraternity complain that it is becoming increasingly difficult to find free-parks. The relentless development of the Spanish coast has all but halted free-parking and put pressure on the places that remain. Large numbers of motorhomes can test the local community, this doesn't mean you'll be moved on every night. Even if you are, this process is very civilised and polite, and by no means aggressive. To be honest you're better off staying in the campsites, and only free-parking when moving around or for the experience.

Cold wintering

The colder European countries can be wonderful in the winter. It is an excellent time for city breaks and a surprising amount of campsites are open. (The Caravan Club Europe books have a clear map showing in red which sites are open). The camper-stops and free-parks are quiet as are the tourist sites.

Temperatures - Most of Northern Europe experiences snow, so it can be cold even in southern parts of France or Northern Greece. You can ski in Southern Spain, on the Sierra Nevada, Sicily, on Mount Etna, and in Northern Greece. Eastern Europe is extremely cold due to the Siberian effect and in January and February expect temperatures of -10°c in the day and -15°c at night, though -21°c is not unusual.

Skiing - Wherever you ski there will be somewhere to stop over night. Camper-stops and campsites are available at large and small ski resorts in Germany, France and Italy, but only campsites in Spain. The Alps can be busy and expensive; the Pyrenees offer cheaper alternatives but it's not worth visiting the Balkans or Scandinavia. If you are determined to ski, it can be very enjoyable and cost effective; consider waiting for March, when the weather begins to warm up.

www.motorhome-list.org.uk has a good article detailing skiing with your motorhome under the heading 'travel info site listings' which also details campsites and camper-stops at ski resorts.

Heating - Keeping warm is a top priority, and your motorhome will need to be kept warm too. Without mains electricity it is possible to stay still for two or three days whilst using lights and constantly running the blown air heating. With electricity things are a lot more comfortable. We have discussed the merits of an oscillating fan heater before but here again they have advantages. They usually have two heat settings, they distribute heat around at floor level, and they can be used to warm up or defrost a specific area. Finally, they help to prevent cold corners where condensation may collect. When using electric heating in freezing conditions it is still necessary to run the blown air system to keep lockers and pipes warm, although it may not be necessary to run the gas heating.

In winter we rarely use electric hook up, instead opting to use our gas heater to keep us warm. In Bulgaria and Romania, the gas heating was left on day and night when stationary. Advice from the National Caravan Council, www.nationalcaravan.co.uk Tel:01252 318251, is that the gas heating system should not be used whilst asleep at night, due to concerns that vibrations from travel may have dislodged vital components. All but the oldest leisure vehicles have systems that draw and exhaust air from and to the outside. The heater therefore works like a radiator. A heater that has not been serviced for years may increase the risk of internal carbon monoxide release. A properly serviced heater and an audible carbon monoxide detector should reduce the risk. Ventilation is vitally important, the practice of covering vents to reduce draughts is potentially life threatening when using gas. Lastly there could be a gas leak but LPG has a stench agent added so careful checking before going to bed is essential. In severe snow/blizzard conditions the level of snow may need to be monitored to ensure adequate ventilation around air intake and exhaust. Roof exhausts can have manufactures' extensions fitted should this be a risk. Prevention of snow building up under the motorhome may be necessary.

In our Hymer cold temperatures were of little problem because of its German standard of winterisation. Our Swift is said to be suitable for all year round use but we have found some flaws. There is no blown air heating therefore the lockers and bathroom become extremely cold and pipes could freeze. The fridge cabinet is not a sealed unit and has unbelievable draughts. The Haynes *Motorcaravan Manual* and *Caravan Handbook/Manual* explain this scenario also providing a diagram of the correct installation.

According to John Wickersham the author of the books who also wrote the installation manual for Electrolux now Dometic says it is also responsible for poor fridge operation. The fridge in our Swift doesn't cool properly and has the giveaway symptom of a warm draining board during operation. The grey waste tank is slung under the body and will freeze. The gas locker holds two 3.9/4.5kg bottles which are simply too small if relying solely on the gas heater. Ideally the locker should hold at least one 11kg bottle. The final major issue is the close proximity of the heater to the rear bed, it is conceivable that bedding could catch fire whilst asleep. See gas and carbon monoxide alarms in ***Chapter 4***, detailing a safe three-way solution.

Engine condition - Ensure your engine is in good condition, including battery, antifreeze, screen wash, thin oil for cold use - consult your manual. Engines that are worn will be very difficult to start. In very cold temperatures you may have no choice but to use an 'easy start' spray (if in doubt carry one).

Fuel (diesel) - Diesel can freeze, to prevent this manufacturers add special antifreeze. Continental fuel stations sell diesel for use in varying cold temperatures, this is clearly indicated on the forecourt. Once in the cold countries it shouldn't be a problem, but if you depart the UK having fuelled up in the Summer, the last time you used the motorhome, and ascend the Pyrenees in freezing conditions you will incur problems. Diesel fuel filters collect water that naturally occurs in fuel tanks, this water will freeze and can prevent fuel reaching the engine. It is easy to check as most filters have a hand tight bleed off at the bottom, a couple of anti-clockwise turns is normally enough. Truck drivers and farmers often fuel up at the end of the day, this stops condensation forming on the inside of the empty fuel tank.

Snow chains - These are a legal requirement in most countries and essential in snow or ice. Don't even consider not purchasing them as they could save your life. They are widely available on the continent and you will need to get the right ones for your wheel size. They cost around €100 and are easy to fit, though it is worth practising as the weather may not be that pleasant when you need to fit them for real. It is a really dirty job due to the grit on the road, it can also be wet and cold so a sturdy pair of waterproof gloves are essential.

Motorhome cab screens - Below is a guide to making cab screens, all the materials are available cheaply in the UK and across Europe. This design has been tested effectively to -21°C. A new loft insulation that looks like silver bubble wrap is now available from DIY stores and builders merchants in the UK, it is rated to be the same as 50mm/2" of polystyrene. These instructions will make three individual sections, which attach to the inside of the cab windows with suckers. You will need some bubble wrap, double sided sticky tape, gaffer tape and suckers.

Measure cab side windows and windscreen, both vertically and horizontally

For each window cut out 1- 3 layers of silver/bubble wrap to size, insuring the smooth side is outermost.

Stick layers together, using double sided sticky tape, ensuring taped vertically and around all edges. Taping vertically stiffens them up so they stay in place better.

Cut small slits in the bubble wrap to attach suckers, once you have decided where to fix them. You will need at least four suckers, one from each corner, possibly eight for the windscreen.

Fit the screens and ensure they fit before trimming and gaffer taping edges to keep out moisture and add durability.

Keeping clean and storage- A plastic stiff bristled brush (part of dustpan set) is invaluable to brush shoes and jackets covered in mud and snow. Also a box lined with newspaper for shoes kept by the door helps keep the motorhome clean. Walkers and skiers should consider where they will store this equipment at the end of a day's activities. Skis and boots may be stored in the bathroom while they dry out, but long skis may not fit. Caravan style porch awnings provide useful storage space and help reduce draughts through the door. If an awning is used then snow will have to be dusted off regularly to prevent the awning collapsing.

Additional considerations - Carpets make a big difference preventing cold coming up through the floor. Shutting off the cab, the coldest part due to windscreen heat loss is also helps. Those with drop down beds in the cab may consider a different sleeping arrangement away from the large, cold cab windows.

Hot water bottles and extra duvet/blankets are essential for keeping warm at night, as are slippers when lounging.

Leaving your motorhome unattended in the cold - When leaving your motorhome unused all liquids must be drained off, black, grey and fresh water, including all pipes, as much as possible. Opening all drain valves and taps then driving up and down steep hills is a good way of emptying pipes. Remove all liquids and foods that could spoil or split and remember to drain your water heater, toilet flush and remove your water filter!

Getting to your destination

European roads vary widely, although investment by the EU has improved many countries' roads. The Caravan Club Europe book is essential as it gives detailed, annually updated information on road speeds, driving regulations, such as dipped lights at all times, and road signs.

Maps

Investigate and purchase maps before you leave, as outside of the UK it is difficult to find maps that show the minor roads in any detail. The opposite is true in Germany where maps are so information packed they become confusing. General European tourist maps normally detail scenic routes, thermal waters or places to visit, useful when route planning but country maps usually contains much more detail, allowing easier navigation. Although computer software is useful guiding you from A to B be careful not to miss interesting routes. When purchasing maps try to buy book style, as fold out maps can be unwieldy and long term use can cause them to tear along the folds. Fold out maps tend to be cheaper, smaller, lighter and are often given away free by tourist information, details in ***Chapter 9: Country Guides.***

Www.thewrinklies.co.uk wrote: We are continually amazed that the navigation system can put up with our unscheduled diversions up side roads for coffee, into supermarkets for food etc. If you divert from the calculated route, the voice nags at you to 'turn around when possible' for a few minutes then you can almost hear a resigned tone in the voice as it says 'recalculating route'. Strangely, if you come upon a new stretch of road that the map does not know about, it says nothing, just shows your position marker out in the boondocks.

Driving distances

Europe is not as big as it looks and it is possible to drive from Bari in Southern Italy to Calais in two days. If you are intending to head to Nordkapp (Europe's most northern car park) remember it is a very long way north, followed by a very long way south, with little motorway.

Legal requirements

Many countries require the following items to be carried in a vehicle; first aid kit, fire extinguisher, red warning triangle (2 in some countries), reflective jacket, spare bulb and fuse kits, spare driving glasses, euro plates or GB sticker.

Alcohol - In most European countries the legal level of alcohol in blood/breath is significantly lower than the UK. Several European countries have a zero tolerance to alcohol. It is recommended that no alcohol is consumed if you intend to drive. The Caravan Club Europe guides detail specific information. Remember that alcohol consumed the night before may still be in the system, so leave plenty of time before driving.

Speed traps - Many countries use speed guns to catch speeding motorists, followed by on the spot fines, the Greek police excel at this. A vigilant motorist will notice that oncoming vehicles usually flash to indicate the presence of a speed trap.

Road Conditions

Road conditions in Europe are good on main routes, and outside of major cities roads are generally quiet.

Toll Roads - Toll roads are common in Europe although quiet and quick they can be uninspiring, and the expense of using toll roads soon adds up. Unfortunately signing is often confusing and can mislead you onto a toll road you didn't intend to take, so extra vigilance is needed when following a road that runs parallel to the toll road. Maps identify toll roads so check the key. Be aware there is a time limit on some toll roads. In Portugal you must exit the toll road within 12 hours, 24 hours in France, failing to do so may result in additional cost. We strongly advise against spending the night in a motorway service station because of the risk of theft and the possibility of overstaying your welcome.

Mountain Roads - Mountain roads are excellent for getting off the beaten track, offering incredible beauty and awe-inspiring views but don't expect them to have crash barriers. Expect the unexpected such as animals on the road, or subsidence, causing the tarmac to become very bumpy and in worst cases slipped away. Hills and hot days can cause a bit of a stink inside the motorhome as smells are released from the drains. Prevent this by plugging all drain holes so the smell cannot escape.

Your motorhome will probably be loaded near to its designed maximum laden weight. Engaging mountain journeys with an

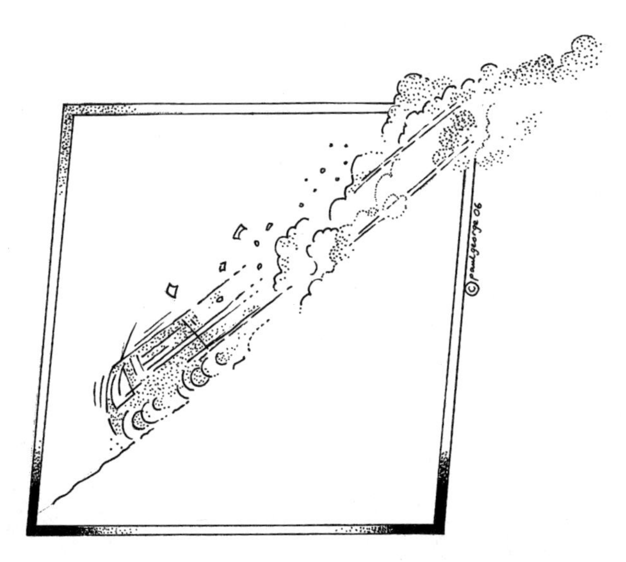

'Controlled descent preferable'

overloaded motorhome and heavy trailer will not only cause unnecessary strain, it may not make the steeper climbs.

Steep hills are marked with a triangular road sign, the pictogram identifies "up" when the slope is to the right (/) and "down" when reversed to the left (\ ). The angle is either marked as percentage i.e. 25% or a fraction 1 : 4 this would be very steep, for every 4m forwards you go up 1m. The most important driving skill is a controlled descent to avoid 'brake fade'. This phrase does not put enough emphasis on a truly horrifying experience of discovering that your brakes no longer work. When descending down miles of mountain road more braking is inevitable. Used excessively, the brake pads/shoes and disks/drums become extremely hot, this heat alters the characteristics of the compounds resulting in friction being lost and therefore reduced breaking. The warning signs are a strong chemical smell similar to burning electrics or metal being cut by an angle grinder. The next stage is smoke coming from the wheels although it may be too late by then! Pulling over and allowing brakes to cool should make them function again, however they should certainly be inspected if they reach the smoking stage by a qualified engineer and probably need to be totally renewed. The golden rule is descending a hill in the same gear used to ascend, in reality second and third gear is used most, but sometimes first is appropriate. Automatic gearboxes have the same function simply taking the lever from drive to the appropriate gear, speed must be reduced before doing this. Selecting low gears allows the engine to do most of the braking. Excess speed will still have to be controlled by braking, but do not rest your foot on the pedal it is better to brake harder periodically. Do not worry if you are holding up traffic, take your time and pull into a lay-by when possible. A consequence of road straightening is there are normally lots of lay-bys. We have a passion for driving in the mountains and always choose the scenic route, we had no problems and had no need for repairs or parts required after 27000 miles.

Rain - Beware driving in the rain when off main routes, not all countries have effective road drainage leading to flash flooding and hazardous conditions due to minor land slips. Driving through deep puddles with dubious contents is stressful and in most cases unnecessary.

All countries endeavour to keep the main routes open in winter with grit and snow ploughs, although snow chains may still be required. Minor roads may not be maintained so stringently. Ensure you are prepared for every eventuality if you deviate off the main route or there is any possibility of a navigation error (easier and more dangerous than you may think).

Our diary reads: ...it was a normal wet day by UK standards but it appears that in Sicily they simply have no drains. This means the water rushes off the hills from the farm tracks, bringing rubbish with it, and gushes down the road making driving treacherous. At one point the police had to stop us in a tunnel as rocks and plants were dropping off the entrance and exit, it wouldn't have been too bad but water was coming through the tunnel joins too.

Driving at Night

Driving in the dark on domestic roads can be difficult as pedestrians often use the hard shoulder as a footpath. This is especially common in Eastern Europe where unlit roads and pedestrians wearing black can make it a truly terrifying driving experience. Frequently unlit vehicles, including horse-drawn, will be travelling against the traffic flow.

Lights – Unless you have an unaltered import your headlights will be set up for the UK and illuminate to the left more that the right. Beam benders are basically little stickers placed on the lights to prevent dazzling oncoming drivers, which on the continent will be on your more illuminated left hand side. Some motorhomes may not be able to use these so check first to see if other adjustment is required. As you are unlikely to drive much at night it is not worth permanently changing your headlights to suit the continent, but foreign importers will probably have spare headlights. Buy at least two sets of beam benders before you leave (they fall off), even if you find some for sale on the continent they are the wrong way round.

Flashing – Although the Highway Code describes flashing fellow motorists to be used as a warning, being flashed in the UK usually means a motorist is giving way. On the continent it is definitely intended as a warning. Never pull out in front of a vehicle that flashes you as it is probably travelling at great speed and is not going to give way under any circumstances. A car driving with lights on when such is not required could also be indicating the same thing. Never make assumptions.

Other road issues

Towing - Some scenic routes are unsuitable for vehicles towing and the alternative route, sometimes indicated by a car and caravan, should be followed. Consider keeping a sign in the cab depicting a motorhome and trailer so other motorists understand that you are towing and may suffer difficulties reversing.

Capital cities and large towns - Avoid driving into large cities where possible, as they can be busy, confusing and stressful experiences. Is it really worth the double parking of Rome and the chaos of Athens when you can park outside the town and use public transport to get in?

Ferries

Across the channel - There are various options for crossing the channel, including the channel tunnel. Contact The Motorhome Ticket Club, The Caravan Club, The Camping and Caravan Club or The Motor Caravan Club all of which offer members discount ferry trips, it might be worth becoming a member for the discount. See club section in *Further Information*. Consider travelling on strange days to unusual places, such as Harwich to Hook van Holland (6 hour crossing) on a Sunday, which may be considerably cheaper than Dover to Calais. Always check if the destination country is on public holiday as you may struggle to find a campsite. Details of public holidays are detailed in the Caravan Club Europe guides.

Europe - Ferries are common across Europe, thankfully you are unlikely to encounter another as expensive as the channel. It is worth thinking about using ferries as opposed to roads as they may be cheaper given the fuel and time taken to get somewhere. Always ask if you can camp on board which means staying in your motorhome as opposed to having a cabin. This is cheaper and a fun experience open to motorhomers. Electric points on deck are common so plug in your electric cable to run the fridge as the use of gas is strictly prohibited. Sometimes these are located in the deck roof and staff lower them with a pole, on other ferries they are on the walls. Gaffa tape may be needed to stop the cable becoming a trip hazard. Those not keen on ferries, should avoid the fjords area of Norway as roads end abruptly and a ferry is needed to continue the journey - this can happen several times a day, fun but hard on the budget.

The ferry experience is normally confusing but never more frantic than in Greece where you may be asked to reverse on or off a ferry. Be aware of grounding when entering or exiting and be vigilant for other motorists or pedestrians.

In Italy and Greece, especially out of season, timetables at small ports should be treated more as guidance than fact. Tickets for long crossings can be purchased from brokers before the ports, or on board for short trips.

> Our diary reads: Woke up at first light aware that at any moment a ferry might appear on the horizon. The ferry never arrived and by 3.30 – when we'd been guaranteed a ferry - we gave up waiting and asked. The ferry wasn't coming but it was sailing at the other port along the coast. So we drove to that one and arrived at what appeared to be total chaos with little ferries turning up everywhere, and everyone bundling on – no ticket office or destination sign. Apparently they all went where we wanted so we pulled onto one with inches to spare.

Repairs

Continental campsites out of season are ideal for checking over the motorhome. Usually there are people willing to lend a hand, tools or advice. Cleaning a vehicle inside and out is the surest way to find any wear and tear. There are plenty of accessory shops and garages across Europe for major problems. In France and Germany some leisure vehicle dealers have camper-stops adjacent, so you can order and wait for spares and repairs. Repair jobs in Scandinavia are very expensive, as are oil changes in Italy. If you think you are going to change your own oil check the sump plug before departing, as many cannot be undone with a spanner but need a key. There are no camping shops or dealers in Greece so you may have to think around an issue, water pumps, for instance can be obtained from a boat or marine shop.

The Motorcaravan Manual by John Wickersham published 2004 by Haynes - An essential guide for potential and current motorhome owners. The book discusses everything from purchasing to detailed chapters on motorhome maintenance, including bodywork, gas systems and upholstery. Those intending a long trip or tour should consider taking a copy to aid general maintenance and repairs.

Hitchhikers

Before picking up a hitch hiker it's worth considering the implications it may have on your journey. As well as the dangers associated with inviting a stranger into your home, will they harm you, damage any property, invite themselves for lunch or decide that they like travelling by motorhome and not want to leave, especially if you have a spare bed? You may end up transporting illegal immigrants especially if you intend to cross a border.

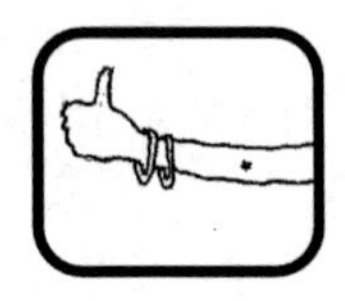

Www.thewrinklies.com reads 'On the way up to North Cape, we relaxed our usual rule and picked up a hitch-hiker, complete with around 100kg of back pack and assorted dangling things. He turned out to be a Finnish student. We stopped so Mother (Anne) could have a smoke and when he got back in, he slammed the door so hard he wedged the fly screen part of the door so I could not open the door any more. I think the shock also dislodged one of the grilles over the fridge vent, because at the next smoke break about two hours later we noticed a great yawning cavity which had previously been neatly covered by a plastic grille. ...Anyway, we deposited him at North Cape, for the next hour or so we kept dodging and hiding so he did not play the sympathy card and try to beg a bed for the night. He would have had a job pitching his tent in the car park as it was rock and gravel. About 9.30pm we saw him hiking off southwards again. We thought that was the last we'd see of him. Next morning, about midday and 100km south of North Cape, we came round a corner and there he was with his thumb out! We immediately initiated an animated conversation which involved looking anywhere but forwards, until we were well past him!'

Further Information

Caravan Club Europe Guides provide detailed information on legal requirements of individual countries including international road signs and speed limits.

AA www.AA.co.uk provide information for driving in Europe, including toll information.

www.ideamerge.com/motoeuropa provides detailed information on individual countries and the camping section is quite useful providing some information on free-parking.

Cons and tricks

Fire!

On the coast road between Southern France and Northern Spain, motorhomers have reported a fire hoax. Smartly dressed men and in a reasonable car, frantically wave and point at the rear of the motorhome. Having encouraged the driver to stop they pull in behind and get out to identify the fault. A lit oily rag is thrown under the motorhome, the smoke and commotion is designed to get the occupants out, so a companion can rob valuables or steal the motorhome. The only advice that can be given is, if you think it's a trick it probably is, so making it obvious that you're not an easy target is your best defence. You may try getting a passenger, if you have one, to lock all doors and windows whilst still moving. Also they should sniff around the back of the motorhome as the smell of hot brakes or burning rubber is very obvious. Check mirrors, look out of the windows, see if other motorists are looking at you strangely, and switch on your rear view camera if fitted. Give the suspects the international OK sign and beckon them to go on their way. Filming or photographing them, and making it obvious will probably work. Remember, most mobiles now have cameras so any small object will look convincing. What ever else you do, don't pull over until they, and any other suspect cars, are well away.

Parking security

At tourist sites you may be asked to pay security/parking by an unsavoury character or child. This is a scam where you are paying them presumably not to damage your vehicle. It is up to you whether you pay or take the risk. Just try not to let it ruin your visit, and report it if possible. This only happened to us in Sicily at the Valley of the Temples.

Being followed

In capital cities, towns and tourist sites it is possible that you could be followed then mugged or pick-pocketed. Always be aware of your situation, especially people brushing up against you, or engaging you in conversation, asking directions, for change or a light. If you feel someone is in your personal space, step away and don't feel embarrassed about offending them. Always present yourself as an unsuitable victim. Bags should be firmly attached, either as rucksacks on both shoulders or strapped across the chest. Rucksacks and bum-bags are especially vulnerable in crowds. If you need a handbag use one with a strap that can be placed across your chest, keeping the bag in front of you. Keep all cards and spare cash out of sight, in a money belt, also keep a mugger's wallet (see below) in a zipped pocket. Do not take or wear expensive jewellery unless you are prepared to lose it. If you think you are being followed, stick to populated areas, vary your walking pace, stop to look in shop windows. Try to deter your follower and get them in front of you and if necessary go into a café or get into a taxi.

Checking forgeries

Should you ever be asked by official looking people to have your money checked, as there has been a spate of forgeries, don't fall for it. Simply say you will call at the police station.

Remember these attacks are rare and unlikely to happen if you are vigilant.

Personal Security

Muggers wallet

This is a simple system of having a fake wallet that is carried with you at all times. Make the contents look as real as possible, out of date or cancelled credit cards, a photo, some receipts, business cards etc. Have a small amount of money in it, enough to get you through the day or top up when in a secure location. Always use this wallet otherwise it won't be convincing, additional money and cards can be kept in a hidden place. If someone attempts a mugging they have something to steal that you are prepared to lose, hopefully it will be over quickly and no harm done. The same wallet should be left out at night for the same reasons. A fake set of keys could also be left out with a branded ignition key, which could be bought, from a scrap yard.

Money belt

Used in conjunction with the muggers wallet, these belts are usually flesh coloured with a zipped pocket. They are very discreet when worn around the waist, under clothing and out of sight. When out and about most of your cash along with passports, cards etc should be carried in the money belt.

Magic whistle

A useful trick if you lose each other or you are alerting your partner to a concern you may have. Simply decide on a code whistle or song, which is used for these occasions, when you lose each other or feel alarmed simply whistle, or sing the song to alert your companion. A little embarrassing at first, we always use it in the supermarket, not because we feel we are being robbed but somebody always wanders off.

Weapons

It can be tempting to carry some kind of defence, such as pepper spray or a baton. The problem with weapons is they can be used against you, as well as the legal implications, so do not be tempted to carry any.

Isolation

Isolation can be a problem for trips longer than four months, even if you travel as a couple. It's easy to spot the sufferers, as they tend to jump out of their motorhome, no matter how cold, eager to speak to anyone with a British number plate. Presumably this happens to other nationalities as in remote places everyone appears to be the best of friends. The symptoms are easy to diagnose as sufferers have to talk at you for around ten minutes with tales of great finds and break downs before they are capable of a two way conversation. To help keep the isolation at bay it is good to socialise and information swap whenever possible.

Brit hunting **-** This simply involves wandering around the campsite, looking at the number plates. Once you find a British one you simply knock on the door and introduce yourself. This may sound a little imposing but most people are more than happy to chat and swap information. But its biggest gain is for your mental health, it really is good to talk. Sometimes a simple wave from an oncoming British motorhome is exciting. Identifying number plates is hard and it would be much nicer if everybody had a GB sticker on the front, as well as the back of the motorhome.

Socialising **-** Socialising is a big part of being away, be it with the locals or other campers, it can lead to some great evenings and cause you to take a new direction. All you need is a bottle and some bottle - thankfully one normally brings the other. Non-drinkers will find having a book to swap or any other spurious excuse like "I don't suppose you have a widget like this one" also works well. Most people are happy to chat whether they are touring or static. Once a cyclist chased us down as we entered a large Spanish wintering site, we managed to shake him off but later found him in a rally tent when we were Brit hunting.

International Relations **-** Don't be put off if you don't speak a foreign language, with a little time and effort you can still have some good times and excellent experiences with the natives or other nationalities. Try to say something in their own language even if it is only 'hello' ('hallo' in German). It's good for people to know who is in your motorhome as they may act as your security. Chances are you'll end up bumping into some motorhomers again.

> At a camper-stop in Germany we met a couple in a VW motorhome. They spoke good English and we talked until the small hours. We swapped emails for several months and six months later they were kind enough to let us have some insurance documents sent to their house, which we picked up when we passed through.

Information sharing - Information from other motorhomers can lead to great experiences or avoid difficulties. Whenever there is potential for swapping info take a general map of Europe, and a pen so you can write the information directly onto the map. You are guaranteed to come across it at a later date if you decide to travel in that area or country. You're bound to be told about horror rumours, so negative comments should be evaluated on their merits.

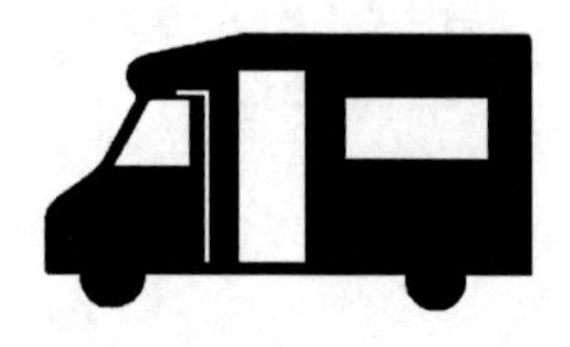

Chapter 8 - Entertainment

When you're not driving what do you want to do? Your hobbies and interests will influence when and where you go. The longer you are away the more important this becomes, preparing entertainment is as important as preparing your motorhome or paperwork.

> Www.thewrinklies.co.uk reads 'Not much to report, still sitting here on site in Barcelona, twiddling my thumbs and trying to make jobs last twice as long. ... Because I was bored yesterday I investigated the water connection adjacent to our pitch. ...Without thinking what I was doing I poked a screwdriver into the connection and received a copious supply of water straight down my front. Water pressure is about 80psi so after I moved out of the jet it soaked not only our washing but next doors as well! Ho hum!'

Weight should be the first consideration for everything you pack. Work out what you are going to use and when. You simply can't take everything.

Books

Go go motorhomer have you any books?

Yes sir, yes sir, three full nooks!

One for the driver and one for the dame,

And one for the motorhomers driving down the lane.

The books, magazines and newspapers you take away for your two week holiday will be really appreciated by long termers. Even if you don't meet any please leave them at reception or in the toilet block. English language books are available across the continent, with the biggest range in capital cities. As these books are expensive, it is far cheaper to swap books with fellow travellers. This is a standard practice abroad and a great way to meet people. Taking a guidebook detailing the history of the area you're visiting may help with the enjoyment of the trip and provide interesting information on how the country evolved.

Remember books are heavy so you wont be able to take many!

Entertainment from electrical items

The following items can be run on the mains, through an inverter from the leisure battery or off the 12 volt system.

Television

If you intend to only take a television abroad then make sure it is one compatible with the European signals, it is unlikely that the one you have at home is. Ideally it should also be able to operate on both 12v and 240v so it can be run without an inverter, thus less draining on the battery. These are widely available as are flat screen monitors that weigh about half that of a conventional TV. Further information on portable televisions is available in the Caravan Clubs leaflet (free to members) entitled *Portable Televisions*. A high gain aerial will be required both in the UK and abroad to ensure good reception. Several countries have some programmes in English often films with the subtitles in that country's language. In addition various in-car portable DVD players are available. A third option is using a laptop to play DVD's, and watch both local and satellite TV. See 'laptop computers' below.

Satellite TV

A good way of keeping up with the news and weather, very occupying on wet days and on campsites when you have mains electricity. It is surprisingly easy to set up. You need to purchase a dish, cable to connect the dish to the satellite receiver box, a scart lead to plug the satellite box into your television, a tuner so the satellite signal can be found and a compass so you know which direction to aim the dish. In addition you will need to acquire a viewing card to decrypt encrypted channels that are not 'free to air' which is inserted into the satellite box.

- *Free to air* As the name suggests these are free and can be picked up without a card and by non skyboxes but must be digital, some of which run on 12v. The BBC TV and radio channels are available as are news programmes from SKY, ITN and CNN. Other channels include Men and Motors, Extreme Sport, You, Performance, Classic FM TV and many more including lots of radio stations. If you can live without the other channels and are visiting the near continent a 12v box is probably the best option as most channels are broadcast by Astra 2D giving the smallest footprint (area where signal can be receive) that just spills over the channel.

- *Sky* If you are on subscription and wish to keep it going whilst you are away this may prove a problem, especially if you are contracted to keep the box connected to a phone line. The only thing you can do is to speak to Sky, and make sure you don't contravene your contractual agreements. The copyright on Sky cards only allows use in the UK and Ireland, but are free to be used anywhere within. Some contracts require users to keep the skybox plugged into a phone line for 12 months.
- *Freesat* A new development now available from Sky with no subscription. This card has a one off cost of £20 for which you receive 120 channels including all the terrestrial broadcasts.

Dish options - fixed or unfixed

There are two options either, one fixed to the roof of your motorhome or a freestanding version, utilising a tripod, and a very long cable.

- The unfixed version has the advantage that you can move the dish around once you have parked the motorhome. This is a good system if you intend to stay on one pitch for some time. Ensure you have a long cable, as the ideal location for the dish may be some way from your pitch. It is acceptable to have your dish off your pitch as long as it's reasonably sited, reception is a conundrum for all nations. The problem arises when in transit as the dish needs to be stored so locker space needs to be found, many opt to attach the dish to the ladder.
- Fixed versions are the tourers ideal solution, as the dish is securely mounted to the roof it is useable at camper-stops or free-parks. Due to obstructions; trees, sun shades, and buildings it can be difficult or impossible to get reception. People can be observed performing what has been described as the 'dance of the satellite' jigging around the pitch to get the best position for the dish - providing better entertainment for onlookers than satellite itself! The dish can be manually elevated, self seeking or

using the Camos satellite dome can be used on the move, the latter costs £2000 and is available from Roadpro who say it performs as well as an 85cm dish.

- Tabletop versions are suitable in good reception areas and can even be used through the window. A good, low commitment dish for UK and near continent users.

Reception

Good reception is all about preparation.

- As the dish must not be obstructed it is worth walking the site with a compass to select a pitch with the best reception potential.
- It can be difficult to get reception in bad weather, so you may need to wait for it to pass before you can lock in to the satellite signal. If you are already locked in strong wind may require slight adjustments if the dish moves. Rain and snow affect signal strength and snow on your dish is a problem.
- Satellite footprint - this describes the area in which the signal is intended to be received. You need to consider where you intend to travel, as the Astra satellite footprints are not intended to cover the whole of Europe. This said, a two metre diameter dish with a high quality LNB Low Noise Block will pick up the Sky broadcasts well outside its footprint maps. With an ordinary roof mounted dish you will struggle to get reception in North Norway, Southern Greece, Sicily, Southern Spain, and Eastern Europe. To overcome this you could buy a large 1.2m diameter dish which helps in the more difficult areas. We received signal through our roof mounted Katherin square dish but only Channel 4 in the Lofoten islands (Astra 2A/ north) and in Sicily, Greece and southern Spain some of the free to air channels, (Astra 2A/B south. The BBC and ITV stations are currently broadcast free to air from Astra 2D this has the smallest foot-print and is centred roughly on Chester.
- Initially you will be given a code to enter into the digi box to receive programmes, this code does change so it is worth chatting to other Satellite users to exchange codes as some work

better than others in different places and the more codes you have the more chance you have of a better reception. Follow the set up instructions to bring up the signal strength and lock indicator. The signal strength will show any satellite it is receiving whether or not it is the right one. Visit www.ses-astra.com for a comprehensive list of extra channels and codes. This page also describes the installation process for up to 50 extra channels.

- Finding the satellites soon becomes easy, first adjust the elevation, the information is supplied with the box. In Norway the dish is nearly straight up and down in Sicily the dish will nearly collect water. Then adjust the LNB skew left or right again information is supplied. Finally aim the dish to the east and adjust the satellite finder so its not squeaking and no lights are on. Now turn the dish slowly to the right you will pass over some weak signals, when you reach 28.2° east on the military scale or 158° depending on which you prefer to use, the finder will go off the scale. It is possible to turn the finder down to fine tune. Fine tuning can also be done up and down if necessary. After a few seconds delay the signal strength and lock indicator on screen should come up. We have known this take a while on the outskirts of the footprint but once it does that's it although you may wish to remove the sat finder. Someone will always offer to help if you are having problems.

240v and 12v

Satellite can be used both when hooked up to the mains and when free-parking by using an inverter. A 110Ah battery will provide an evening (about 3 hours) of Satellite TV, although you will need to drive or hook up to electricity the next day to recharge.

Further Information

A wealth of information can be obtained from

- www.satelliteforcaravans.co.uk which provides detailed information including dish sizes which have been effectively used in Europe.
- The Caravan Clubs leaflet (free to members) entitled *Portable Televisions*

- Road Pro, a company that specialise in 'practical products on the move' sell satellite systems, provides useful information in their catalogue and are very helpful both over the phone and at their premises. Tel: 01327 312233 or visit www.roadpro.co.uk
- Sky provides information on what channels are available on which subscriptions. Tel: 08706 061111 or visit www.sky.com
- BCC Prime is a special service run for ex-pats and designed for use abroad. A different box is needed as it tunes into Hotbird 6. This is a pay to view encrypted service. More information is available from www.bbcprime.com
- Information on the ASTRA satellite services is available from www.astra.lu
- Information on channels and footprints visit www.satcodx.com

Satellite TV changes constantly, as ever this information is as accurate as possible but please make further inquiries before investing in a system. We will keep up to date information on our website.

Laptop computers

There are many types of small computers available that can store vast amounts of information. It is worth taking a computer and digital camera to store photos and save on the cost of development, which is expensive in Europe. Modern laptops have vast memories and can store music, audio books, maps, tourist information, book text, languages courses, play games, films, play DVDs and CDs which are available in English across the continent. Digital and analogue TV can be received and played on a laptop by slotting in a card plus a small aerial is also available which has many features including recording a different program to the one being watched. Internet access is available and discussed in ***Chapter 5 communication by phone and email***. Satellite navigation is also possible see ***Chapter 4 Extras and add ons***. All the laptop gadgets are available from www.action-replay.co.uk . If you are considering purchasing a computer it is worth doing so before you depart, as electrical items are no cheaper on the continent and software can be loaded and information from the internet can be downloaded before you depart. A whole host of information can be stored at no extra weight. They are economical on 12v and can provide unlimited information and entertainment. For us, an essential, and even if you have never used a computer it would be worth attending some classes to make use of this fantastic facility.

Previously mentioned in ***Chapter 4*** are laptop safes available from Argos. Laptops have a small hole about the size of a grain of rice that is where a 'Kensington lock' attaches. A wire hawser is used to secure the laptop to any fixed object, the front seat bases are ideal. The hawser looks like a dog lead with the Kensington lock on one end and a loop on the other so going round the object and through the loop is enough.

Radio

Unfortunately getting the world service abroad can be quite tricky so it is worth contacting the BBC before you depart to obtain a list detailing the frequencies on which World Service is broadcast. Satellite tuned radios are available which should help. There are dozens of local and national radio stations included on satellite TV.

Water sports

If you are the active type taking a water sport item is a good idea. There are plenty of accessible rivers, lakes and seas that can fill your time, and the Europeans are streets ahead of the British at enjoying these facilities.

Swimming

Is an ideal pastime and can also provide a much needed cool down or wash! There are excellent swimming facilities in the lakes and fjords of Sweden and Norway, often with changing rooms, toilets, barbeque sites, wooden piers and diving platforms all available free of charge. Even high in the Artic Circle this water can be warm. Italy is perhaps the worst place to go for a beach holiday as most of the beaches are private and only small areas are public, often in the most inconvenient place. Although you can pay to visit a private sector, if you visit out of the main season it shouldn't be too problematic. In addition to a swimming costume,

take water shoes (diving suit material with rubber soles), which are excellent and available from virtually every seaside town.

Snorkelling (scuba diving)

A simple but effective way of enjoying the water, lakes and rivers and can be just as exciting as the sea. Snorkelling kits are available from many UK supermarkets and Argos and take up little space or weight. It is worth doing some research before you go away to find the best spots and times of year to visit to avoid disappointment. If you are into scuba diving then prior research is essential.

Fishing

Can be cost effective if you manage to catch your supper, sea fishing is free and no licence is required. Fishing is so popular that every single tourist information office has details on localities and bait shops, but check before fishing lakes and rivers, as a licence may be required. Scandinavia has excellent fishing in the rivers, fjords and sea. The Lofoton Islands are a good place to head if you're a keen sea angler and fancy catching month's worth of fish in a day. Take a rod, capable of catching 30lb fish, also pack lures for cod and cole fish. Most European rivers and lakes offer good fishing although keen sea anglers may struggle in the Med. We advise that a light spinning rod and a selection of lures is the most practical and entertaining. Snorkelling in rivers and lakes is a good way of picking up spare tackle, and is great fun.

Boats

Are readily available to buy in varying sizes and guises. Some motorhomers tow a motor or sail boat behind them whilst others opt for the fold out or blow up variety. It is worth investing some time to get the right item for you. A windsurfer may be more practical than a canoe if you intend to spend more time by the sea and vice versa if you want to be inland. Alternatively you can hire boats wherever you are as long as you are in season (June-August). As with all water sports it is important not to overstretch your capabilities and have the necessary training and insurance. When taking your boat abroad contact the Royal Yachting Association Tel: 08453 450400 www.rya.org.uk as qualifications and ownership documents may be required.

Where do you put your keys/phone?

Consider taking a waterproof pouch if you have an electronic key fob or don't want keys to suffer water and salt corrosion.

Ball Games

There is often time for a quick game in the evening, this can not only be pleasurable but can also develop into a social event. Many of these games are ideal if children decide to visit.

Boules

A great motorhome game, although the metal version weighs about 5kg. Ideal for any ability, many campsites have boules courts or have roads surfaced in a light gravel which is an ideal playing surface. This game breaks language barriers better than any other and can be played individually, in pairs or teams. Boules can be purchased from a variety of stores in the UK and France.

The basic rules. – (Two to four players)– Equipment; three boules per player, one puck and a tape measure (also needed in toolbox). Start at one end of the court, Player 1 draws a circle in the ground big enough to hold two feet. Player 1 then stands in the circle and throws the puck, no less than five metres away. Player 1 then throws their first boules, the idea is to get as close to the puck as possible. The throws can be through the air or rolled along the ground but must be under arm - the palm clasping the top and the fingers gripping underneath, apparently it is all in the wrist action! Player 2 then stands in the circle and throws their boules, it is legal to knock out the opponent's ball or the puck. If playing on a court then a ball is disqualified if it hits the edge or back. The player with the boules furthest away from the puck throws again. This continues until no boules are left. The player with the nearest ball wins and can score up to three if all boules are nearer. The winning player draws a new circle no more than a metre away from the puck and the next game starts back the other way. Continue playing up and down the court until one player reaches 13 points and has won.

(For up to 12 players) - Each player has one or two boules depending on numbers and are divided into teams of two or more. Substitute player for team above and play the same rules.

Please note these are only basic rules and more can be learned from watching the French who play it absolutely everywhere in the summer. Don't confine the game to gravel, it is equally good on grass, tarmac and sand though the boules behave slightly differently on different surfaces.

Frisbee golf

A very simple game ideal for high energy people and children. Requires one Frisbee per person. Decide on a course where the Frisbee must hit, go through or land on at least three items, i.e. through the gate (over wont do), land on the bench and hit the gate post. Each item needs to be at least ten metres apart (though the course can be as big or small as time and space allow). Each person must complete each obstacle and count how many throws it takes. The winner takes the least amount of throws to complete the course. Not only is this enjoyable it can be used to make a walk more interesting. If you don't have Frisbees, balls or sticks work too.

Golf

There are numerous excellent golf courses across Europe so it is worth taking your clubs. Either play as you go or research which ones you wish to visit before you leave the UK and plan your trip around them. Nearby campsites may be able to offer discounts. Remember if you take your clubs they will be heavy.

Tennis

Many campsites have tennis courts and users of Camping Cheques or Camping Card International sometimes get discounted rates. If you are an avid player it is worth taking your kit with you, if not you can often hire equipment on site.

Badminton/volley ball/football

Beach versions of these games are played right across Europe in the summer (June-August), although you may need to access them on a private beach. Taking your own equipment is probably worth while if you can't live without it.

Arts and crafts

Any arts and crafts should be considered as they are generally light weight and very time consuming, below are some examples

Painting and drawing

You are never short of something to draw, either from life or a post card. Art material can be found cheaply at The Works chain of High Street shops or Argos, and even if you have never drawn before there are a range of books to get you started. An ideal hobby for occupying your time, both in the motorhome, or out and about.

Photography

Excellent hobby to record the trip as there is always something to photograph. Developing photographs is very expensive abroad even over several days so consider using a digital camera. Purchase enough memory cards or a laptop to keep your pictures on. Lonely Planet book *Travel Photography* details how to take good pictures.

Needle point/crochet/ tapestry/knitting

A popular hobby among female motorhomers, done while co-piloting now sat nav has taken over from map reading. Visit craft shops before you depart to stock up on equipment but remember it may become all consuming, it is good to look out of the window sometimes.

Outdoor Pursuits

Walking

An excellent, virtually free activity. It is worth taking some proper walking boots or sandals because even if you just intend to visit tourist sites in a town it's amazing how long you can be on your feet and being comfortable is essential. Also in Italy and Greece you may be literally climbing over the ruins so good footwear helps you keep your grip.

If you are a serious walker then take your poles, compass and consider a GPS system that you can use in your motorhome and out walking. Germany and Hungary provide some good walking information but for other countries gather information in the UK as it is difficult to get, let alone in English and Ordinance Survey style maps can be impossible to find. The Czech Republic and Slovakia have multiple walks of varying lengths, clearly signposted.

Scandinavia has some fantastic long walks of three or more days. If you wish to do these and are only away for a month to six weeks consider not taking a motorhome at all and simply put your pack on your back. There are plenty of free walking huts to sleep in, then use public transport to get back.

The Lonely Planet produce walking guides for countries in Europe, offering walks with good descriptions and simple maps varying from three hours to several days. Those focusing on France try the AA guide *500 walks in France*. This is a large heavy ring binder featuring walks from one to 12 miles but has quite detailed maps and instructions that can be removed to walk with. www.walkingworld.com provides information for walking in the UK and Europe. Membership at £17.45 allows access to walks and maps across the UK. The book, *Walk Europe*, discussed on the web site, may be a worthy book to purchase.

Cycling

If you are fairly active a bike is a good option whether you tour or stay still, and always excellent for getting to the shops or the bus stop. Holland, Germany, Denmark and Hungary are excellent cycling countries with plenty of cycle routes. Copenhagen and Stockholm are ideal cities to explore by bike. Other countries are more mountainous and accessibility depends on the fitness of the cyclist, although all countries are mad about cycling so spares and repairs are easy to get. Bikes are available to hire in most places but if you want to take your own consider a hybrid bike - basically a cross between a mountain and road bike, which gives you ultimate flexibility. Holland has some excellent bikes not seen in the UK. You will need at least 10 gears, a bike with only three will only be good in Holland and Denmark. Couples with different cycling abilities should consider a tandem as the stronger cyclist will help the weaker and will not be constantly waiting. Once again look for cycling information in the UK.

We had already decided to go for a cycle and an English couple told us Pisa was only four miles away so we decided we would go there. After about 6 km we came to a sign saying Pisa 14 km! Hardly four miles! We decided to keep going as it was on the flat. Pisa was fantastic. We were really tired by the time we had cycled the 20km back, but the English couple did buy us a much-needed beer as an apology.

Discovering Germany by Bike is a publication available from the tourist office. It contains details of cycle paths across Germany and is designed for all cyclists as it lists routes, tourist information and accessibility. *Cycling around Hungary* is a guide with 100 tours and a 1:250000 map of the country. This multi lingual publication (English, Hungarian and German) is available from bookshops in Hungary.

The website www.cycletourer.co.uk details cycling across Europe. Also worth a visit is www.nationalcyclenetwork.org.uk and the European cycling federation http://www.ecf.com/index.htm.

The Baltic States of Latvia, Lithuania and Estonia are also good for cyclists, as they are mainly flat with light traffic. Some tourist information should be available but cycling is not popular in all the countries so you may need to make up road routes yourself.

Skiing

Almost every country in Europe has ski slopes - obvious exceptions are Holland and Denmark. Many resorts in France, Spain, Italy and Germany have campsites and camper-stops nearby. It is easy to hire equipment at the slopes. If you do plan to ski then the *Good Ski Guide* gives you an idea about resorts. If you search hard enough you can find some relatively cheap, quiet resorts undiscovered by package holidays. Stick to Spain, France, Germany, Italy and Greece, as Eastern Europe and Scandinavia are extremely cold, especially in January and February. ***Chapter 7*** details skiing with your motorhome. Also see www.motorhome-list.org.uk.

Fauna and flora (free food)

Identifying the wildlife, flora and fauna can be very interesting. There are many books available on this subject and can give even a complete novice a lot of fun, as can finding free food and trying a local speciality, such as cloud berries in Norway - a type of raspberry. Europeans really love gathering free food so there should be plenty of people to ask. If you gather mushrooms in France take them to the Chemist to get a second opinion. Campsites can produce oranges, olives and pine nuts.

Collins produce a bevy of useful books for enjoying wildlife and fauna in their *Natural Guides, Wild Guides* and *Pocket Guide* series including titles: *Butterflies and Moths, Birds, Trees, Mushrooms and Toadstools.*

For free food Richard Mabey's *Food for Free* 2001 edition contains photos and explanations of edible food and Peter Jordan's *Mushroom Picker's Foolproof Field Guide*. Be sure any food you have gathered is safe to eat.

Food and Drink

Food and drink is one of our favourite elements of travel, but

proves disastrous for the payload both motorhome and personal. The obvious countries to visit are France, Germany, Italy, Spain, Greece and Portugal. Denmark and Belgium can tempt any sweet tooth. Eastern Europe also offers some delightful specialities; you certainly won't starve in Hungary. Wine lovers can go to any of the numerous wine producing countries. Many camper-stops are at vineyards, and large or small wineries are usually happy to open their doors to any passing traveller for a taste and opportunity to sell. Expect to find good wine for sale for 1€ per litre in supermarkets, and from 1-3€ in cantina, little wine shops found in most towns selling locally produced wine. The UK, Ireland, Denmark, Belgium, Germany, Czech Republic and Central

European countries are famed for their beer and lager. It is possible to stay at pubs in the UK and Germany. For those who like something stronger there are ranges of spirits produced, some more delightful than others, and tasting of these is possible in the appropriate areas. The Lonely Planet produces *World Food Guides* for some European countries.

Beach combing

Simply walking the beach looking at the sand for coins, and objects of interest. In the Autumn this can be a rewarding process. More enthusiastic beachcombers may wish to purchase a metal detector. Soaking coins in vinegar can clean them.

Tourism

It is quite easy to plan a whole trip around tourism. A general guide of Europe should ideally be read in advance as this will highlight the best bits and give you an idea of where you want to spend your time. Try to remember it is not a competition and you really don't have to see everything. Often the best parts of the trip are not Florence or Rome or Paris but the sleepy town where you drank with the locals. To avoid the crowds and meet the locals, it is worth travelling out of season.

In France, Germany and Italy you could easily spend a year in each country, but guidebooks help you choose where to go and what to see. We found both the Lonely Planet and Eye Witness guides very good.

It is possible to suffer 'tourist fatigue' where you simply see so much that everything looks the same or at least you saw a better one in another country. So if you are planning a trip of more than four months (what we believe to be the optimum travel time) try to break up the tourism with other hobbies.

Guidebooks

The Lonely Planet produces guides that cover sections of Europe that you may wish to focus on, providing a general guide to a selection of countries. The *Mediterranean* guide would be useful for any beach babes or sun seekers. Those wishing to travel in France, Germany or Italy the individual country guides are better. Although in Scandinavia the general guide is enough. Lonely Planet's *Europe on a Shoestring* has some suggested tours from two weeks to two months, these may prove ideal if short of time or wanting to follow a recommended tour. Also included are details of campsites and restaurants. Visit www.lonelyplanet.com. For those who simply can't decide where to go try *1,000 places to see before you die - a travellers life list* by Patricia Schults. It covers the whole world but 342 pages cover Europe.

Driving guides

- Thomas Cook produce a series of *Driving Guides*, which cover limited areas of selected countries these won't be very useful to those on longer tours.
- The AA *Best Drives* cover a variety of countries, these are designed primarily for car drivers and no campsites are listed.

Card/board games/jigsaws

Table games can provide excellent evening entertainment, or on wet or cold days, take some even if you don't play them at home.

It is worth taking two packs of cards as they can provide games for one or more people and offer excellent value for weight and space. Invest in a good card book for variety. At campsites it is possible to organise games evenings.

Hamlyn's *Complete book of Card Games* would be worth packing.

Games while driving

On long drives games can provide a lot of entertainment and conversation, also helping with driver fatigue.

I-spy

You may think you grew out of this game as a child but even if there are no kids in the car it can be ideal for keeping the mind active and entertained.

Spot

First person to spot three items i.e. post box, green car and a bakery. You can get quite imaginative such as a kite, golden eagle and a hobby (may take some months).

Straw Poles

Fun and informative. Co pilot notes numbers i.e. favourite colour of car in Greece, types of cars in Germany (interestingly mainly German built), or nationalities of trucks on the road.

Word association games

For example 'knives you don't sharpen' answers butter knife, fish knife, Stanley knife, etc. Any statement will do, general or specific, do you know all the Shire counties in the UK?

Music and Audio books

These can provide excellent in cab entertainment. Audio books are now widely available at book shops.

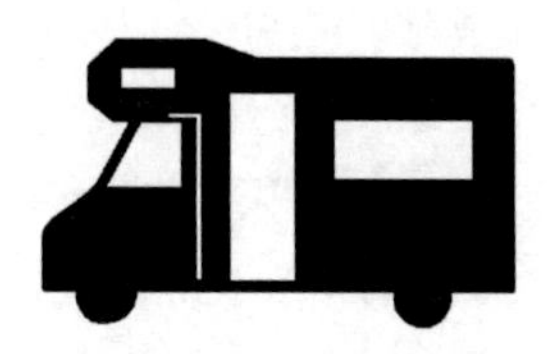

Chapter 9 - Country Guides

Save time and money by gathering tourist and campsite information before departure. Planning a route and itinerary will allow adequate equipment and provisions to be sought. It can be very difficult to acquire useful literature in English whilst away.

Each mainland European country has been listed detailing what to expect and where good information can be gained. Where possible websites have been listed so information can be gathered en-route, or better still collected/downloaded before leaving.

Good tourist information leaflets are listed under each country, and are available free from the address given. Many of these are excellent with detailed road maps, scenic routes and campsites, often providing better information than retail publications.

Information on the internet in a foreign language can be translated. One way is to search for them through the search engine Google www.google.co.uk and click on the option 'translate this page'. The English is sometimes a little interesting but generally makes sense.

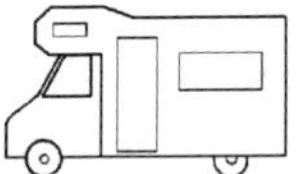

Andorra

Known for its duty free but not as cheap as you might like. Very busy in the Summer and Winter. Andorrans speak Spanish and French. English is widely spoken.

Accommodation

The motorhomes at the borders do appear to be free parking for multiple nights. Campsites are equivalent to the rest of Europe and are expensive.

Driving and Roads

The roads are good and there is no real need to go through the toll tunnel in the summer. In towns there is no motorhome parking, the confusion and officious traffic wardens will result in a visit to a campsite, even if you just want to stop off for an hour. To avoid this join other motorhomers wherever you see them parked. Fuel is very cheap.

Time of year to visit

Late Spring and early Autumn should see the least crowds. Those wishing to ski will have to do battle in the Winter when snow chains are essential.

Tourist Information

Andorran Delegation, 63 Westover Road, London, SW18 2RF Tel: 020 8874 4806 www.andorraonline.ad

Things to do - shopping

Everyone seems to go shopping crazy in Andorra, inspired by duty free prices. Locally grown tobacco, and medication, (often free from prescription restraints), are cheap, other items, may not provide the bargain you're looking for.

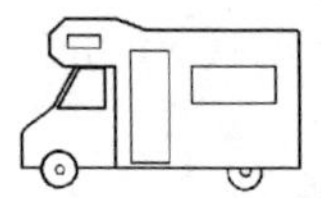

Austria

A beautiful mountainous country ideal for summer visits when it is hot without being scorching, or those wishing to ski in the Winter. Visitors may find it pricey though fuel is cheaper than Germany.

Accommodation

The tourist office produce a fantastic leaflet *Camping and Caravanning* with a detailed road map on one side and information on campsites on the other. This also states 'Except in Vienna and protected rural areas visitors are permitted to sleep in camping vehicles outside camping sites. But local restrictions can apply, and campers are not allowed to set up camping equipment beside their vehicle'. Additional information on campsites is also available from Camping and Caravanning Club Austria www.cca-camping.at and the Osterreichisher Camping Club www.campingclub.at .

A range of campsites and camper-stops are detailed on www.bdauncey.ic24.net and Austrian camper-stops are also detailed in the German book Bord Atlas.

Driving and Roads

A vignette sticker, available from garages around the border, is needed to travel on the motorways. For a motorhome 3.5t and under it costs around €7.60 for 10 days, €21.80 for 2 months or an annual sticker can be purchased. Those in motorhomes over 3.5t are charged by the km, prices vary depending on the number of axles. A Go box needs to be acquired instead of a sticker, this box calculates your distance. Don't think you can get away with using a sticker as motorhomes are generally weighed. This also means 3.5t rated motorhomes that are overloaded may be fined. More information is available from www.asfinag.at or contact the tourist office and visit www.go-maut.at for a route calculator.

Time of year to visit

Austria is a year round destination, with the summer being best for alpine scenery without the snow, and the winter for snow sliders.

Tourist Information

Write to: Austria Info Holiday Service Centre, PO Box 83, A-1043 Vienna, Austria. Tel: 0845 101 1818 or visit www.austria.info/uk.

Things to do - Walking

Walk Austria Magazine, available from the address above details 8 walks, mainly circular achieved in a day. The magazine recommends walkers join the UK branch of the Austrian Alpine Club for mountain rescue, contact: AAC, 2 Church Road, Welwyn Garden City, AL8 6PT.Tel: 01707 386740, www.aacuk.uk.com. This club also sells maps at the scale of 1:25,000.

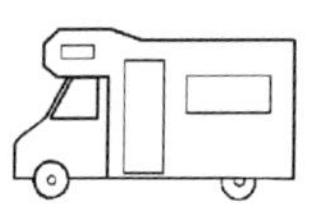

Belgium

A little country often overlooked by motorhomers entering or exiting from France or Holland. Famous for chocolate and good for seafood this country is well worth a detour.

Accommodation

Belgium has 800 campsites. 250 campsites are listed on

www.campingbelgique.be. The *Wallonie Camping Guide*, available from the tourist office, lists campsites and farms. There are a few camper-stops in Belgium, www.bdauncey.ic24.net lists them along with campsites. It is possible to stop by the side of the road for one night.

Driving and Roads

Belgium has good but busy roads, prone to heavy traffic around Brussels and Antwerp. Belgium is small and it takes just over three hours to drive its length.

Time of year to visit

Summer is the best time to visit but early autumn and late spring should also be good.

Tourist Information

Regional tourist information is available from Belgian Tourist Office for Brussels and Wallonia, 217 Marsh Wall, London, E14 9FJ www.wallonie-tourisme.be or www.belgium-tourism.be or www.belgiumtheplaceto.be. Alternatively you can call Tel: 020 7531 0390

Things to do

Three things stand out when looking at the tourist information, first battlefields, second breweries and beer cafes and third chocolate factories and shops. All of which have brochures available from the tourist office.

Bulgaria

On the motorhoming frontier passed through either into or out of Greece/Turkey. Not an easy country to motorhome in, though it is possible to pass through in a day.

Accommodation

Bulgaria has very few campsites with suitable motorhome access, as camping involves tents or hiring a wooden hut. TIR parks will charge you a minimal amount to stay, and there is often a shop, shower and restaurant for the truckers. You are unlikely to be disturbed in town squares or car parks.

Driving and roads

The main route through to Greece has been vastly improved for the Athens Olympics so you can now drive through in a day. To ensure slow speeds in built up areas and villages the road has not been improved, if you don't slow down don't expect your vehicle to survive. The route to Turkey is well used by truckers and in reasonable condition. On minor routes the roads are axle breaking and in really rural areas are simply mud tracks. In built up areas roads can be very narrow and power lines can be low. Don't be surprised to share the road with transportation pulled by animals.

Time of year to visit

Outside of the summer months Bulgaria can be a difficult place to visit. Those wishing to ski should not consider Bulgaria a viable option due to extremely cold temperatures, lack of campsites or camper-stops meaning there is no mains power. Bulgaria has become increasingly expensive around ski and tourist resorts and dual pricing is a tourist policy.

Tourist Information

www.bulgariatravel.org This country is presently outside the EU.

Things to do

See the Rila monastery, drive through the Valley of the Roses and drink the local brandy it's very good. The Black Sea resort is just starting to grow so a peaceful time out of season could be had.

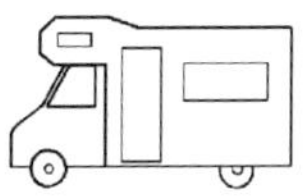

Croatia

Believed to be one of the most unspoilt countries in the Mediterranean. Anyone looking for the idyllic Mediterranean, should visit soon just in case the developers move in.

Accommodation

There are 526 campsites, over 100 have 1,000 pitches or more, most campsites are open from the beginning of April to mid October, with a few open all year. The *Camping and Caravanning Guide* available from the tourist office gives an overall view of what to expect and contains details of 131 large campsites and lists 365 mini camps with 30 pitches maximum. There are 17 naturist beaches and 12 naturist sites. Further naturist information is available in the tourist office publication *Naturist Campsite Catalogue*.

For those wishing to free-park, the Croatian guide to Camping and Caravanning states 'any form of camping in free areas outside registered camping sites, or parking areas for caravans and motorised campers is forbidden and is punishable by law.'

Driving and roads

The *Croatian Tourist Map*, available from the tourist office, one side it details tourist information the other details roads, including town maps and campsite identification. This should be enough for motorists.

Time of year to visit

Most campsites are open from April to October, and being a beach holiday destination visiting in these months will allow swimming in the sea.

Tourist Office

Croatian National Tourist office, 2 Lancasters, 162-164 Fulham Palace Rd, London. W6 9ER Tel: 0208 563 2616 www.croatia.hr This country is presently outside the EU.

Things to do - beach holiday

Relax and enjoy the crystal waters and soak up the sun on the beach. The *Hiking Tracks and Promenades for the Kvarner Region* available from the tourist office contains walks from 30 minute town walks to long mountain hikes.

Czech Republic

Situated in the centre of Europe, the Czech republic has witnessed many episodes in Europe's history. The country is rich in historic sites as well as outside activities.

Accommodation

There are around 560 campsites in the Czech Republic detailed in the *Camping Road Map,* available from the tourist office or visit www.camp.cz. 20 Small farm sites are detailed in the *Rural tourism guide in the Czech Republic*. Free parking is illegal.

Driving and roads

A sticker, vignet, needs to be purchased to use motorways. Details for motorists are on the *Road Map,* from the tourist office, which is sufficiently detailed to be used as a main map and contains information on vignet prices.

Time of year to visit

The Czech Republic is a year round destination, especially to those wishing to have a city break. Although quiet in winter it can be cold and should not be attempted without a fully winterised motorhome.

Tourist Information

Czech Tourist Authority, UK & Ireland, Morley House, 320 Regent St, London W1B 3BG or visit www.czech.org.uk or www.czechtourism.com call Tel: 0207 243 1115

Things to do

Prague, the capital, is renowned for being one of the most beautiful cities in Europe. Those who enjoy lager won't be disappointed, as 'Bud' and 'Pils' brand names originate from here. Why not combine the two and have a lager in the capital.

Denmark

With CL style camper-stops and a variety of campsites, the flat terrain of Denmark offers a low level snap shot of Scandinavia, though food is still expensive.

Accommodation

There are around 500 campsites in Denmark, some operate a camper-stop system for motorhomes that arrive after 8pm and depart before 10a.m. Visit www.danskecampingpladser.dk for camping information.

Denmark has Certified Location style camper-stops, which have limited facilities. The *Camper Guide Danmark* produced by DACF details sani stations, farms, camper-stops, campsites and community spots through out Denmark. This book can be difficult to find in the country itself, but if you hunt hard enough you may find one. Alternatively visit www.dacf.dk before you depart which details where it is available in the English section. Don't expect site owners to speak English but they will be more than happy for you to stay. According to the Danish Camper Guide book it is possible to free-park.

Driving and Roads

Roads are good but due to the geography of their country (flat as a pancake) it can be difficult in wet, windy weather. The country consists of one section connected to the mainland, and two islands connected by a toll bridge. One fun diversion if you're prepared to take the risk is driving on the beach.

Time of year to visit

Weather in Denmark is similar to the United Kingdom and therefore is an ideal summer destination.

Tourist Information

Visit Denmark, 55 Sloane Street, London, SW1X 9SY
www.visitdenmark.com or call Tel: 020 7259 5959. The *Denmark map*, available free from Visit Denmark, detailing roads and campsites should be enough to get around.

Things to do - cycling

Denmark is an excellent place to cycle, with flat, quiet roads and cycle lanes. If you plan to cycle while you are away Copenhagen is well worth a visit. The town has special cycle lanes with their own traffic lights and both cars and pedestrians have to give way. Even if you don't own a bike they can be hired for a deposit from bike racks. More cycling information is available from Dansk Cyklist Forbund (Danish Cyclist Federation) www.dcf.dk or Tel: +45 3332 3121

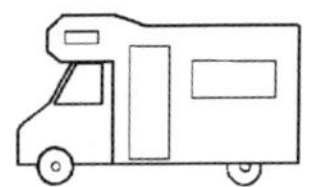

Estonia

Estonia provides a quandary for touring motorhomers. The North East Border with Russia provides an option to visit St Petersburg, if visas allow, and the possibility of driving to Finland. Alternatively a visit to the Capital Tallinn can be followed by a short ferry to Helsinki, just 80 km across the water. The addition of the Baltic states to the EU has provided a larger loop to those touring Scandinavia.

Accommodation

70 campsites and holiday villages are listed on the Estonia tourist information website. More campsites specify tents than caravans. The website also contains a wealth of good tourist information

Driving and roads

Roads are good, with light traffic. As Estonia is one of the smaller European countries nothing is far away.

Time of Year to visit

Due to its geographical position it would be advisable to visit only in the late spring and summer months as temperatures drop to -8 in winter. The country is prone to showers.

Tourist Information

www.visitestonia.com or www.tourism.ee

Things to do

Bird watching is very popular, and Estonia has many feathered visitors so it is a good destination for ornithologists.

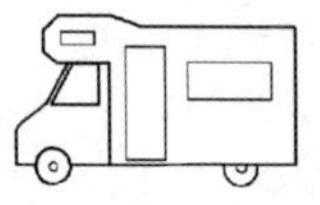

Finland

Unlike the rest of Scandinavia Finland uses the Euro. Often overlooked by motorhomers Finland provides an interesting culture, but beware the mosquitoes.

Accommodation

There are no camper-stops in Finland but plenty of campsites to suit all pockets. Often quiet, picturesque locations. Visit www.camping-total.de/service/continent for details of sani stations in Finland.

Driving and Roads

Reindeer are a real danger on the roads of Northern Finland. They have no road fear at all and are quite happy hanging around on them. Beware any reindeer on the edge of the road and slow down as beeping your horn makes no difference. The main roads in Finland are good, although they may be being resurfaced during the summer months so expect road works and the road surface to be removed.

Time of Year to Visit

The summer is the best time to visit, as winters are extremely cold and have short hours of daylight.

Tourist Information

www.visitfinland.com or call Tel: 020 7365 2512. *Finland facts and map* has a very basic map that you can survive with and some basic information about Finland.

Things to do - driving tour/fishing

Request the ***Touring in Finland*** brochure for scenic drives or visit www.visitfinland.com/touring. The tourist office can provide plenty of information on Fishing. For outdoor activities try www.cyclinginfinland.com and www.hikinginfinland.com

France

An excellent country to visit with a variety of options for motorhomers; camper-stops, France Passion, and a variety of campsites to suit all budgets as well as a wealth of historic sites to visit. Increasingly British products are available but are expensive.

Accommodation

The 11,000 French campsites offer a wide variety of choice, from big commercial to farm to naturist. Municipal campsites are a good option for people on a budget. All campsites range in condition, and the star system provides little help, so it is worth investigating before you book in.

France has thousands of camper-stops called 'Aires', some even offer free electricity. These are detailed in several 'Aires de Services' books available at supermarkets in France and from www.Amazon.fr, The Camping and Caravanning Club and The Motorcaravanning Club. *The Official Guide Motorcaravan Tourist Stop Over* and *Le Guide National des Airs de Services Camping Cars* are written in French but easy to understand. There is also a map that can be purchased but this does not contain as much information as the books. See ***Chapter 8: Accommodation***, for more information. These books are published annually in the Spring and sell very quickly. Free-parking is permissible in France.

Driving and Roads

Toll roads exist all over France and these are generally quiet and useful if you are in a hurry, however the minor roads running parallel are good and interesting. Fuel is far cheaper at supermarkets all of which are clearly signed off the minor roads. The French driving style can be erratic and unnecessary. Two road maps that may be worth purchasing to assist in touring and route planning are *France Routes Historiques* and *Jardins de France* both by Institut Geogra Phique National.

Time of year to visit

France is an excellent destination any time. Years can be spent discovering what this country has to offer. There are always plenty of excellent places to stay.

Tourist Information

French Government Tourist Office, 178 Piccadilly, London W1J 9AL www.franceguide.com Tel: 09068 244123

What to do - Tarn Valley

The Tarn valley is an excellent drive for those of a daring nature offering a wealth of history and outdoor pursuits. Those towing will need to follow the caravan route.

Visit www.autoroutes.fr for information about French toll roads, this information is available in English by clicking on the Union Jack. The monthly magazine *Camping in France* details numerous tourist sites and tours and may be worth while for those looking for annual holiday advice or intending to spend some months in the country. Also visit www.campingfrance.com

Germany

An excellent country full of camper-stops (Stellplatz) and fantastic towns. There are a wide range of campsites for all budgets, a great location at any time of year.

Accommodation

There are 3,500 campsites in Germany, all tastes and budgets are catered for. The camper-stop system is so good it makes Germany an easy, stress free, joy to visit.

An excellent variety of camper-stops are detailed in the publication *Bord Atlas* by Reise Mobil, published annually and available from bookshops and newsagents. There are several other stellplatz books but for non German speakers this one is the best. It covers Germany, Austria, France and Italy in detail plus enough in the Netherlands, Denmark, Switzerland and Hungary to keep you busy, not to mention a splattering in other countries. More details on this book are available in the free-park section, ***Chapter 8***. Also visit www.bdauncey.ic24.net for details of camper-stops and campsites visited by an English motorhomer. Many include photographs. Free-parking is permissible in Germany

Driving and Roads

The smoothest roads in Europe, without tolls, although they are very busy they are still clearly signed. Be aware that beer in Germany can be very strong, 15 per cent is not unusual, so a lunchtime drink could put you well over the limit. A basic road map showing main roads, scenic routes and UNESCO world heritage sites can be obtained from the tourist office, ask for *Germany map*. Those intending to tour the country in detail should purchase a road map. These are widely available in Germany and contain such a wealth of information navigators are prone to overload and may need to lie down!

Time of year to visit

Germany offers much to the motorhomer with excellent camper-stops and campsites plus plenty of tourist sites and motorhome dealers to visit. Every town is worth exploring. The Black Forest is excellent offering wonderful walks in the summer and skiing in the winter.

Tourist Information

The German National Tourist Office, PO Box 2695, London W1A 3TN Tel: 020 7317 0908 www.germany-tourism.co.uk. It is possible to obtain a copy of Camping and Caravanning in Germany but this contains information on some of the commercial sites and isn't very useful.

Things to do - Something for everyone

A variety of brochures to suit all tastes are available:

- *Discovering Germany by bike*
- *Castles, palaces and stately homes*
- *Enchanting little towns*
- *Welcome to wellbeing and spa's*
- *Fascination water - the sea, rivers and lakes*
- *Winter sport info*

- *Europe's romantic castle road*
- *UNESCO world heritage in Germany.*

Greece

A friendly country with some good, cheap campsites but the cost of a return ferry journey to Greece and ferries when you are there may out weigh any savings made. There are no camper-stops or camper accessory shops. Greece is quiet and slightly colder than Spain in the winter.

Accommodation

Greece has 340 campsites, few are open in the winter, although most of these are simply not closed. All sites are quiet with few British visitors. If visiting out of season truck stops are available and Tavernas are often willing to let you stay if you purchase a meal. Free-parking is 'technically' illegal, the website www.gnto.gr states 'wild camping or use of camping accommodation outside authorised camping sites is not allowed.'

Driving and Roads

Roads have been improved due to the Athens Olympics and road signs are in both Cyrillic and English. Motorways around Athens are tolled but other roads are generally good with plenty of ruins for frequent breaks. Few dual carriageways exist and the Greeks adopt a fatalist style of driving, meaning blind bends are equally as good as a straight clear road for overtaking. But thankfully outside Athens the roads are very quiet.

Ferries

In winter, weather conditions make minor ferries more sporadic for island hopping, so be prepared to camp up in the harbour for a few days.

Time of year to Visit

A year around destination. Hot and busy in Summer but quiet and sleepy in Winter. Not suitable for those who want company out of season.

Tourist information

Greek National Tourist Organisation, 4 Conduit Street, London, W1S 2DJ Tel: 020 4959 3000 www.camping-in-greece.gr

Things to do - Tourism

Outside of peak season EU citizens can visit the major tourist sites free on Sundays. The Greeks are some of the most welcoming people in Europe so one of the best things to do is join in.

Hungary

A hidden gem in Europe and an ideal motorhoming country. Tourist information produces an excellent guide to all the campsites in the country. With friendly people the campsites are generally good. A big advantage is many campsites have thermes attached, an excellent way to have a cheap spa holiday.

Campsites

Hungary has hundreds of campsites and excellent tourist information detailing when they are open, their facilities and costs making them easy to find. Many campsites have thermes attached, expect to pay around £10 per night for your pitch, electricity and unlimited use of thermes. Although it's cold in Winter the thermes stay warm making the country a year round destination, something the Germans and Austrians already know about.

Driving and Roads

Although this country is perceived with the Eastern Bloc stereotype it is more like Austria than its Eastern Bloc neighbours. Roads are reasonable and well signposted.

Time of year to visit

Although cold it is not inaccessible in the Winter though due to the thermes it is an excellent location to visit in the Spring.

Tourist Information

Hungarian National Tourist Office, 46 Eaton place, London SW1X 8AL Tel: 020 78231032 or visit www.gotohungary.co.uk

The tourist board produces an excellent publication listing all the campsites in Hungary and indicate whether they have a therme attached. Contact the tourist information and ask for *Camping Map* or pick one up at tourist offices in Hungary.

Things to do - Cycling and Spas

Hungary produces an excellent publication called *Cycling Around Hungary,* not only ideal for cyclists as it also contains tourist information about every town, and the map shows spas and campsites. It is available from bookshops in Hungary and is in English, Hungarian and German. The tourist information office produces a free *Cycling map,* which is very good.

These spa complexes range from communist concrete structures to modern state of the art affairs but don't confuse them with the English alternatives. In Hungary they are inexpensive and used as a social venue by the whole community who chat, play chess or have a beer in the warm water. Although there are over one hundred thermes, the most interesting is Lake Balton, the largest thermal lake in Europe and the second largest in the world. Here instead of simply a plunge pool you enter the lake in the centre of a wonderful Victorian building which you can swim in, under and out into the lake. In the middle of winter in freezing temperatures it is still as warm as a swimming pool. Camping is opposite the lake.

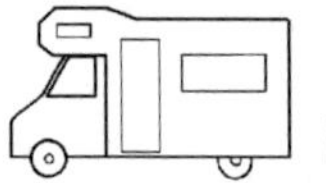

Iceland

On the edge of Europe, the interesting features of Iceland are not widely visited by motorhomers. As Iceland has to import a lot of resources visitors should stock up on food and alcohol before visiting.

Accommodation

There are 125 campsites in Iceland open from June to mid September. The Iceland Tourist Board state on their website 'Camping outside designated areas is not allowed.'

Driving and roads

Iceland has geared itself up for driving holidays, although fuel is expensive so fill up before you go and some roads are unsurfaced. www.vegagerdin.is details road conditions, accessibility and maps with various details.

Ferries

Ferries to Iceland go via the Faroe Islands, the Shetland Islands, or both. So the journey is an adventure in itself. They depart from Scotland, Denmark and Norway so Iceland could be used as an alternative route into Europe. Visit www.smyril-line.com for more details on ferry routes, timetables and costs.

Time of year to visit

Although the Gulf Stream provides cool Summers and mild Winters, as campsites are only open June to September this is the best time to visit, at any time the weather can be changeable. Outside of these months, tourist facilities are known to shut down.

Tourist Information

www.icelandtouristboard.com. This country is presently outside the EU.

Things to do

Iceland is home to the original Geysir, Europe's largest waterfall and the blue lagoon, a large thermal lake. Most towns also have thermal water. Sea angling is good, the midnight sun can be viewed and bird watching enjoyed.

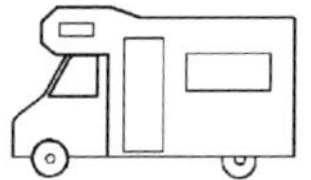

Ireland

The Emerald Isle is a beautifully lush country, steeped in history with a rich culture and welcoming nature.

Accommodation

There are around 200 campsites in Ireland. The Irish Caravan & Camping Council produce a booklet entitled *Caravan & Camping* which contains campsite details 106 campsites and marks them on a map.100 campsites are listed on their website www.camping-ireland.ie.

Driving and Roads

Roads have been greatly improved due to EU grants making Ireland an easy country to get around. As with the UK there are plenty of lanes, but they don't always go anywhere nor are there signs telling you this. The best way to judge these roads is by the grass is the middle, as soon as you see any it's probably time to turn round.

Ferries

Ferries leave the UK from Wales, Scotland and Liverpool. Ferries sail from Cork to Roscoff in France, and from Rosslare to Roscoff and Cherbourg so it is possible to make a circular route, rather than seeing Ireland as a single destination.

Time of Year to Visit

Although it has a mild climate suitable for year round visits, Ireland can be very wet so the summer is the best time to go, but still expect showers.

Tourist Information

Try the websites www.ireland.ie, or www.tourismireland.com. The Irish Caravan and Camping Council produce *Touring guide to Ireland* which has campsite and tourist information. Visit www.camping-ireland.ie

Things to do

Enjoy a trip to the pub, preferably with live music, and enjoy a drink of Guinness or whiskey. Smoking is banned in public areas including bars, nightclubs and restaurants. Information on heritage sites can be found at www.heritageisland.com

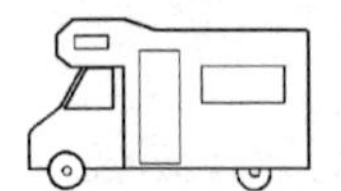

Italy

A fantastic country to visit by motorhome, due to good weather, excellent cultural and historical sites and a wealth of camper-

stops. Campsites tend to be expensive, as are basic provisions of food and fuel. There is so much to see and do you will be spoilt for choice. There is a strong north/south divide and the hotter south is much poorer and has a mafia culture.

Accommodation

Italian campsites are very expensive and if you are planning to tour Italy using campsites alone you will need a serious budget, at least €21 a night. Many sites have very poor facilities, and are un-level. Look out for 'Agro Tourism' signs for cheaper options, or visit out of season using a discount scheme *(See the campsite section of the Accommodation chapter).*

Italy has excellent 'camper-stops' in many of the most famous cities, which provide an excellent insight into Italian culture. Some camper-stop information can be printed off the web. Visit www.camperclubitalia.it/Aree+di+sosta which has the Camper-stops divided into Nord (north), Centro (central) and Sud (south). Details are logged in Counties, such as Lazio, and then provinces such as Provincia di Roma. The camper-stops are then listed under towns in alphabetical order, with directions and facilities listed. Or try www.camper.netsurf.it/ all of this is in Italian. The Reise Mobil Bord Atlas details many of the Italian camper stops, but this is in German. Plein Air publish a guide in Italian detailing the majority of the camper stops but we are yet to find it for sale. Free-parking is permissible in Italy

Sicily There are plenty of camper-stop options across Italy, but Sicily is a little more difficult and free-parking is a necessity as campsites are poor. There are some delightful 'unofficial' free-parks where you can enjoy Sicilian life. Generally the Sicilians are very friendly to motorhomers, and town squares are a good stop, as are fishing harbours. It is important to note that Italians have a cruising culture, where they literally drive around the town in the evenings for around two hours causing major congestion problems. They often end up in the local car park or harbour where the may hang around in their cars and socialise into the night. This can be a little alarming to start with but you'll soon sleep through it.

Driving and Roads

The roads continually deteriorate the further away from the industrial north you get. Motorways tend to be tolled, although the minor roads that run parallel are often more interesting and challenging. Cycling clubs are common and fly along the minor roads on Sundays. Road drainage appears uncommon in Southern Italy which means roads can be filled with flowing water and debris during rain and storms. Road signing can be difficult to interpret so take some time to get it right, a straight on sign often looks to be left or right. The south is less busy than the north but Italians love their cars so there is always some traffic.

Italian Driving style: Don't be put off by the Italian driving, although they have a bad reputation, they have a few rules that can make driving in Italy a little less stressful.

- Italians have two speeds: Fast and slow, those going slowly are happy to drift along and aren't concerned by confused tourists, those going fast are in a rush and drive with full beam or flashing lights, as a general rule everyone gets out their way and lets them though.
- Italians love their horns and have a code: one beep means I'm here. They're not being aggressive but simply reminding you that you're about to reverse into them or they are overtaking you. Two beeps means ciao and they are generally saying hello to someone they know. A progression of beeps or one long beeeeeeeep usually means you're in the way. Either they have nearly driven into you or there is a parked car blocking the route.
- Parking is a sport in Italy and any space is fair game, even if it blocks the road. If parked cars block routes the standard practice is to beep your horn, this results in various shopkeepers and passers by inspecting the situation and then sending a message off to find the car owner, who will then move the car. This stresses no one and the queue of traffic will revel in beeping behind you. it's a cultural thing, and when in Rome there is only one thing to do… join in!
- Tailgating is a source of pride, its just something you have to accept.
- Hazard lights are very useful, when confused with map reading and unsure where to go try your hazard lights, and generally in smaller towns and villages you will be driven round.

Time of year to visit

This is not an ideal winter sun seeking country as campsites are limited and quiet. Southern Italy is more expensive than Spain and in comparison offers poor value for those wishing to stay all winter. Very few British visit at this time of year. Sicily has a small, predominantly German, motorhome community wintering in free-parks. Tourist sites are very busy in the Summer and it can be unbearably hot. Ideal times are Spring, though the sea will be cool, or Autumn.

Tourist Information

Italian State tourist Office, 1 Princes Street, London W1B 2AY
Tel: 020 7408 1254

www.enit.it

Things to do

Tourism is a must, and there is so much to see it can be exhausting just deciding where to go. The Italians also consider their food superior so eating is a must. If you're looking for a cheap meal in Rome find a Chinese. Properties owned by the Italian National Trust (FAI) give free entry to British National Trust cardholders. Contact the Membership Department for details.

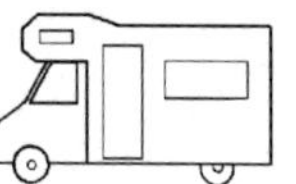

Latvia

Opportunities for a beach holiday with a difference, a chance to branch away form the western Mediterranean and enjoy some of the resorts popular with the Soviets. You may still hear Russian spoken in this Baltic state.

Accommodation

Information on campsites can be found at www.infolatvia.com/category/oldcamping where campsites are listed by region and mainly identify facilities for tents, though some identify caravan spaces. Also try www.camping.lv Many campsites are on the coast, and this is a good place to head for those new to the country.

Driving and roads

The roads are good in this mainly flat country. On major routes petrol stations are open 24 hours.

Time of year to visit

Due to it's proximity to Russia this country is likely to get extremely cold in winter, up to -10°C in the day and -25°C at night. It would be best to visit in the warmest month, July. It starts to frost in September so plan to be heading south by then.

Tourist Information

No tourist office address in the UK could be found. Visit www.infolatvia.com

Things to do

Those not intending to cross the boarder into Russia should visit the town of Krāslava, famed for its Russian and Belorussian architecture. Saunas, called pirts, are very popular and are common across the country.

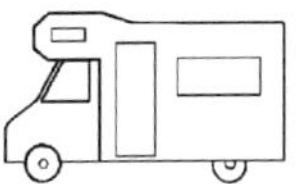

Lithuania

The Baltic state charm of Lithuania has been relatively undiscovered by all but the most adventurous British motorhomers.

Accommodation

There are 33 campsites listed on the tourist information website.

Driving and roads

Lithuania claims to have the best roads out of its Baltic neighbours. Main roads should be fine, but those branching off onto minor roads should take care.

Time of year to visit

Summers are mild and are the best time to visit, providing a break from scorching Mediterranean temperatures.

Tourist Information

No tourist office address in the UK could be found. Three websites should be investigated www.latviatourism.lv, www.tourism.lt or www.travel.lt

Things to do

Lithuania has the smallest coast out of its neighbours, just 90km long. Like its southern neighbour Poland, Lithuania was witness to atrocities of the Second World War, the Paneriai Forest, 10km from the capital has the Museum of Genocide marking the site where 100,000 people died.

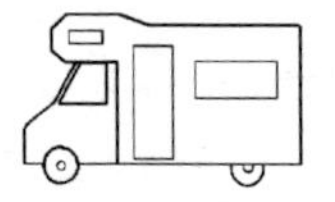

Luxembourg

Although small the Grand Duchy of Luxembourg is worth a visit, encompassing a city experience with the green outdoors in one.

Accommodation

The *camping brochure*, available from tourist information, details 65 campsites. Five camper-stops are listed in the *Reise Mobile Bord Atlas* camper stop book. The tourist information *camping brochure* states 'You are not allowed to sleep in your vehicle on public roads or in public open space'.

Driving and Roads

A country map available from the tourist office, details suggested driving routes, and has places of interest for each route on the back. Ask the tourist office for the *Touristic Map*, who can also provide a map of Luxembourg City.

Time of Year to visit

As with its neighbours, Spring and Autumn would be a good time to visit for a less crowded experience.

Tourist Information

Contact Luxembourg National Tourist Office at 122 Regent Street, London, W1B 5SA or www.luxembourg.co.uk Tel: 020 7434 2800 and request the *Touristic Map*.

Things to do

Enjoy the greenery that surrounds Luxembourg City or tour the Valley of the Seven Castles. Hikers will be in their element as Luxembourg has 500 marked paths totalling 5,000km. Mountain bikers can enjoy 300 km of routes. Maps for these and other outdoor pursuits are available from local tourist information offices or visit www.editionsguybinsfeld.lu

Netherlands (Holland)

A busy, flat country ideal for exploring by bike. With the ease and convenience of the Hook Van Holland ferry port, makes the Netherlands ideal for an annual holiday or relaxing start or finish to any tour.

Accommodation

There are a wide range of campsites available to suit all budgets and desires. The Camping Card ACSI booklet details 89 campsites. Small sites, known as 'Mini Camping', are detailed in *Kamperen op het platteland*, published by Dutch camping association VeKaBo, www.vekabo.nl, is available from bookshops in Holland, but is only in Dutch. SVR, www.svr.nl, is another camping association and members receive a map detailing SVR sites, there is no handbook. Camper Club Nederland, www.campervriendelijk.nl has information specific to motorhomers but is only in Dutch. 22 Camper-stop options are detailed in the *Reise Mobil Bord Atlas*. Occasional overnight parking is allowed in some motorway service stations.

Driving and Roads

Good but busy roads, country lanes can be quiet and narrow. Bicyclists generally have right of way, so drive carefully.

Time of year to visit

The Netherlands experiences similar weather to the United Kingdom so it is best to visit is the late spring through the Summer months. March to May is the season to view the famous bulbs flowering.

Tourist Information

Netherlands Board of Tourism and Conventions, PO Box 30783, London, WC2B 6DH.Tel: 020 7539 7953 or the brochure order line Tel: 0906 871 7777, calls charged 60 pence per minute. A map with main roads and tourist information is available, being reasonable quality but does not contain much detail. www.Holland.com/uk

Things to do

Visit the bulb fields, which flower from March to May. Cycling is the thing to do in Holland as the flat terrain has resulted in a bike mad culture. With plenty of cycle paths the motorhome can be left sited while the country is explored.

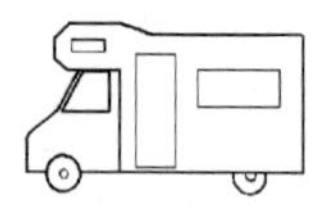

Norway

Expensive, but worth it. A huge country, paradise for those who enjoy the big outdoors. It is expensive, so stock up with food and alcohol, and beware the weather. Norway is a fantastic place to visit and the tourist board provides details of scenic drives.

Accommodation

The 1000 Campsites vary from large commercial sites to plenty of smaller sites detailed in the Caravan Club Europe book or can be easily found. Norway has limited camper-stops, which are called 'Bobils'. Some of these are signed from roads and detailed in the Caravan Club Europe book. Visit
www.camping-total.de/service/continent for a list of sani stations in Norway.

This is a free-parkers paradise. There are some fantastic drives which take you out into the wilds of the country where often free-parking is your only option, but with such a huge migration don't expect to be on your own. The *Norway Facts and Information brochure* states 'It is not permitted to pitch a tent or park a caravan closer than 150m from a house/chalet. Also please note that there are varying by-laws relating to free camping.'

Driving and roads

Not a spare millimetre of tarmac is laid. Dual carriageways are rare and on the northern road only a single lane is provided to pass and re-pass under the railway that crosses the road. Roads end abruptly and ferries are needed to cross fjords, so those on a tight budget wishing to visit Nordkapp should head due north from Oslo to avoid this or drive up through Sweden. Large towns have toll ring roads (the main road) - there are three around Trondheim, which are unavoidable. Just consider it a tax and pay up, driving straight through results in a fine being sent to your home address.

This is far from a cheap driving holiday, although it is a very popular motorhome destination. It is a long way from north to south, although many motorists explain how they enjoy the challenge of the drive. The numerous gravel roads do actually go somewhere and are likely to provide the best free-parking opportunities, as competition is stiff on the tarmac roads. Like Sweden, Norway is probably the safest country to free-park in. We followed a gravel road stopping beside a fjord for three days, only a dozen vehicles passed, the silence was deafening. Maybe this is what people call wild camping however we were still parked in a lay-by. Watch out for moose, although hard to spot these creatures are frequently hit and cause a great number of road fatalities. Motorists are advised to slow down or stop if they see these unpredictable animals.

If you don't want to drive the full length of Norway or wish only to drive one way there is a ferry called the Hurtigruten, travelling the length of the country, stopping at numerous little towns and settlements along the way, providing a totally different view of the country. Consider it the Norwegian bus service. There are height restrictions for vehicles of 1.95 metres on old boats and 2.3 metres on new boats. Visit www.hurtigruten.co.uk or Tel: 0870 7276960.

Time of year to visit

As with the United Kingdom, weather in Norway can be unpredictable. Consider the weather because it could have negative effect on your visit. Norway is an ideal summer location, those visiting in Spring and Autumn may find it cold and roads impassable due to snow. Winter visits should be seriously researched before undertaken.

Tourist Information

Contact Innovation Norway, Charles House, 5 Regent St. (lower), London SW1Y 4LR. The *Norway Road Map* details all roads, campsites and contains information on driving and tourist sites. The brochure ***Norway Facts and Information*** details country information, prices and information on where to take part in activities including glacier walking, water sports and fishing. Both are available from www.visitnorway.com or calling Tel: 0906 302 2003. This country is presently outside the EU.

Things to do - Visit the Lofoten Islands and see the midnight sun

Probably the jewel in the crown of this beautiful country is the Lofoton Islands. High up in the Arctic Circle out in the North Sea they can be accessed by ferry or bridge. These islands offer the opportunity to enter Norwegian society and experience white sandy beaches and crystal seas. Cod liver oil is produced here in the winter along with salt cod. It is an excellent place to see the elusive midnight sun. Motorhomers from all over Europe migrate to Nordkapp (allegedly Europe's most northerly car park).

Poland

Poland has more to offer than a visit to the most famous Second World War Atrocities at Aushwitz. There are plenty of camping options and there should be something here to suit everyone.

Accommodation

There are 500 campsites in Poland rated at 1-3. 1 is the best but probably compare with a mid range British site, whilst category 3 is very basic. Most are open May to September with few open all year. Polska Federacje Campingu I Caravanning (PFCC) publishes *Poliskie Campingi/Polish Campsites* listing the category 1 and 2 campsites. This is available from larger sites or tourist information in larger towns. *Polska Mapa Campingow* shows the campsites and contains details. ECEAT, Polish Agro Tourism, is an option for those wishing to use small sites.

Driving and roads

The main roads are generally good, with country lanes being of varying standards. There is generally a hard shoulder, which slow vehicles pull into to allow overtaking. Avoid driving at night as the hard shoulder/overtaking lane is used as a footpath by pedestrians clad in black, which can lead to scary situations.

Time of year to visit

Poland is very cold and snowy in winter, which can leave it looking bleak and depressing. Visit in warmer months when campsites are open.

Tourist Information

Polish National Tourist Office, 1st floor, Remo House, 310-312 Regent Street, London, W1B 3AX. Tel: 08700 675 101 www.visitpoland.org. Also useful are; www.cycletourer.co.uk/cycletouring and www.ecotraveller.pl which has a map showing campsites.

Things to do

A mini tour of Poland can be made from the Czech republic, as three important and popular tourist destinations lie within close proximity to each other. A few hours across the border Europe's recent past can be seen at Aushwitz. From there head to Krakow, Poland's prettiest town, where there are four campsites. From Krakow visit the Royal Wieliczka Salt Mines, with 350 miles of tunnelling and salt statues, visit www.kopalnia.pl.

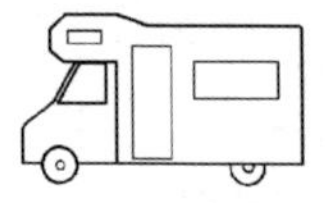

Portugal

This country receives a mixed response from the motorhoming community, some believing it is dirty and below standard and others wondering what all the complaints are about.

Accommodation

Campsites vary in cost and condition, but some are as little as €5 out of season. The publication *Guia Camping*, available from the Camping and Caravanning Club, details campsites in Spain and Portugal, alternatively try www.roteiro-campista.pt. Camper-stops are not common so those wishing to free-park should visit www.campereavventure.it/areesosta-portogallol.htm an Italian site detailing free-parks, sani stations and camper-stops. This information is not known to be in a publication so it is advisable to take it with you.

Driving and roads

As with Spain the roads are generally good although the driving style receives a mixed response. Be careful when travelling on Portuguese toll roads not to overstay your welcome – you have a limit of 12 hours. If you take longer than this you may receive a large fine.

Time of year to visit

Very popular in the winter months with long stay visitors. Extremely hot in the Summer, Autumn and Spring ideal for those who wish to miss the crowds and enjoy the country in good weather.

Tourist Information

National Tourist Office of Portugal, 22-25 Sackville Street, London, W1X 2LY Tel: 020 7494 1441 www.visitportugal.com

Things to do

Portugal is a popular winter sun destination time to sit back and enjoy a glass of port. Alternatively windsurfing and big game fishing are available on the Algarve. Surfing is popular along the

west coast, for more information visit
www.surfing-waves.com/travel/portugal.

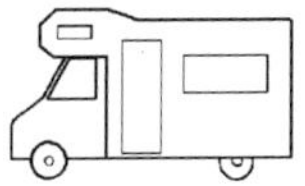

Romania

Increasingly popular with motorhomers wishing to venture out of the European Union. This country is westernising at an increasing speed, though it is still possible to experience the legacy of the Eastern Block.

Accommodation

There are 49 campsites listed on the Romanian tourist board publication *Romania - Motels and Campings Map*. Motorhomers report around five CL style stops, which are signed from main roads and run by Dutch owners. The one we visited was easy to find but was closed in winter. TIR parks will charge you a minimal amount, and there is often a shop, shower and restaurant for the truckers.

Driving and roads

Roads in Romania are reasonable, especially the main truck routes but speed should be used with caution as the roads can hide invisible axle breaking ripples and potholes. In built up areas roads can be very narrow and power lines can be low. Don't be surprised to share the road with transportation pulled by animals. The above publication *Romania - Motels and Campings Map* is suitable to navigate with and depicts campsites.

Time of year to visit

Outside of the summer season campsites are closed. People contemplating skiing, be warned it can be extremely cold due to the Siberian effect. The lack of campsites means that 12 volt is the only electricity supply and it can be very difficult, but less so than Bulgaria

Tourist Information

Contact 22 New Cavandish Street, London, W1G 8TT Tel: 020 7224 3692 or visit www.romaniatourism.com. ***Discover Romania*** brochure has some basic information. This country is presently outside the EU.

Things to do -Dracula

There is a whole range of tourist sites related to Dracula and even a Dracula tour, details available from tourist information. The booklet *Tourist Routes in the Mountains of Romania* has walks with maps and descriptions from a few hours to several days.

Russian Federation, Belarus, Ukraine

It is still a turbulent time in some of the former Soviet states, as alliances change from the old Soviet Union towards the European Union. A visa is required before entering both Belarus and the Russian Federation, but Ukraine has recently relaxed its visa requirements and British citizens can now enter visa free for 90 days. Belarus also imposes fees for drivers of foreign vehicles, so a visit could work out costly. Both Belarus and Ukraine suffered from the Chernobyl disaster, and areas of both countries are contaminated.

Consult the foreign office website www.fco.gov.uk Tel: 0845 8502829 and read their detailed information on visas, licences and road conditions as well as areas to avoid. Ensure that adequate insurance and an International Driving Permit is obtained before you travel. Having said that, these countries are becoming more tourist friendly every year. Those intending to visit these countries will need to be independent and adventurous, not all have campsites of any description. Ideally a visit should take palace in late spring to summer.

At the time of writing the foreign office advise against travel to parts of the Russian Federation. These countries are presently outside the EU.

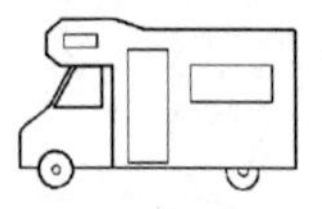

Slovakia

This small country is conveniently situated in Europe. Ideal for a three centre city break, Bratislavia, is a tantalising 30km from

Vienna and Hungary is so temptingly close that Budapest can complete the trio.

Accommodation

There are around 175 campsites to choose from. The Slovak tourist board produce *Auto-Campings - Road Map* which details 78 auto camping sites in the country including addresses and proximity to facilities, such as swimming, skiing (some campsites claim to be just 200m from the ski lift), public transport and mechanics.

Free parking is not allowed.

Driving and roads

The *Auto-Campings - Road Map* is detailed and includes city maps. This should be enough to navigate the country, especially as it also marks castles, spas, hospitals and fuel stations. Toll stickers are needed to use motorways and many fuel stations close after 6 pm.

Time of year to visit

Winters can be cold, but the best time to visit is May and June when it is also likely to be quiet.

Tourist Information

Slovak Republic Tourist Centre, 16 Frognal Parade, Finchley Road, London, NW3 5HG Tel: 0800 0267943 www.slovakia.org

Things to do

According to the website above 'There's a refreshing absence of McDonald's style commercialism that is rampant across western Europe.' But there is an abundance of healthy outdoor pursuits with a wealth of hiking trails, some at high altitude and plenty of skiing in the winter.

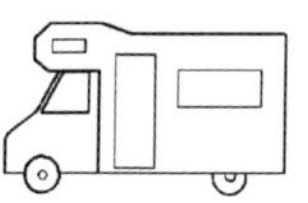

Slovenia

A country the size of Wales, which offers Mediterranean beach holidays as well as extreme sports and skiing.

Accommodation

There are around 50 campsites in Slovenia. The *Slovenija tourist map*, available free from tourist offices, shows campsite locations on a road map. Free parking is not allowed

Driving and roads

Slovenia is 33 km across, so everything should be easily accessible. The *Slovenija tourist map* clearly shows minor roads, campsites, and sites of interest.

Time of year to visit

This is a year round destination suitable for everyone. Those visiting in winter wishing to ski should wait until March to avoid the coldest temperatures.

Tourist Information

Slovinian Tourist Office, 49 Conduit St, London, W1R 9FB or visit www.slovenia.info , www.slovenia-tourism.si for tourist information or call Tel: 020 7734 7133

Things to do

Bled is one of the most beautiful places in Europe and an ideal place to engage in some café culture while you soak up the views. Those interested in extreme sports should visit www.adrenaline-check.com and mountain bikers www.bovec.si and request the *Biking in Slovenia* leaflet from tourist information.

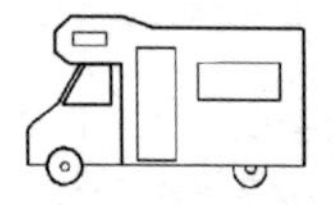

Spain

A popular location for motorhomers especially in winter months, having large sites with facilities for large motorhomes and long term stays. Continual development and the large number of visiting motorhomes makes free-parking increasingly difficult and there are very few camper-stops.

Accommodation

There are 1200 campsites in Spain and the tourist offices fold out *Campings map* shows both campsites and major routes. The Spanish Federation of Camping Sites and V.C also produce a booklet detailing affiliated campsites and their contact details called *Spain Campings*. On the coast there are many large sites available for long term winter stays which can work out to be as little as £5 per night. Many clubs organise rallies to these sites during the winter. The publication *Guia Camping*, details camp-sites in Spain and Portugal, the guide is available from the Camping and Caravanning Club.

Spain is limited to a few camper-stops in the north, for sani stations and camper-stops information visit www.viajarenautocaravana.com/aquiparamos/AquiParamos.asp.

Due to the vast numbers of motorhomers visiting in winter and the huge tourist industry this country is far from free-parking paradise. Don't expect to find an idyllic undiscovered beach where you can live for the winter. The rate of development in Spain means it's hard to find a car park where you can stay for the night without being moved on, although there are a few spots which remain. If you are intent on free-parking in Spain you may find it easier to go inland. The web site www.viajarenautocaravana.com/aquiparamos/AquiParamos.asp has free-parks detailed with directions, cost if any, and when last visited sometimes with a photo - it isn't in English but is quite easy to understand. www.motorhome-list.org.uk details free-parking information in English.

Official free-parking areas can be found in or near some of the national parks. It is advisable to take a supply of water with you.

Driving and Roads

The *Campings Map*, free from the tourist office, is good enough to get by. *The Silver Route*, a leaflet free from the tourist office, details a route from North to South noting the sights of interest. Toll roads exist along the east coast of Spain connecting the popular coastal resorts. Reasonable free roads follow the same route, though signs can mislead motorists onto the toll motorways. This coast can be very busy and is virtually built up along its whole length, there is a good central route that is quiet, beautiful and toll free. LPG could be available at Repsol garages www.repsolypf.com

Time of year to visit

Winter is the most popular time to visit, and sites can be very busy. Spring and Autumn are good times for those wanting to experience the country without the crowds. Summer can be very hot.

Tourist Information

Spanish Tourist Office, 22-23 Manchester Square, London, W1M 5AP Tel: 020 7486 8077 www.tourspain.co.uk. There are many useful publications for each region, those heading south to Alicante should ask for the *Murcia Tourist Map* which details things to do in the area including scenic drives.

Things to do

The Spanish side of the Pyrenees provides excellent walking and skiing all with superb views. Sun seeking motorhomers shouldn't rush through Northern Spain, instead make the most of this fantastic area both at the beginning and end of your visit. This half of the country has the most beautiful scenery, with a very different culture and climate to the south, not to mention the few official camper-stops in the country. The south coast provides the warmest winter climate in mainland Europe enough of a reason for most.

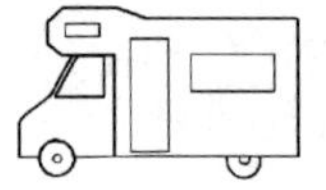

Sweden

Not as dramatic as Norway but just as expensive. The roads are faster and often used as the route back from Nordkapp. Lake Vanern is the second largest in Europe and suitable for those carrying boats.

Accommodation

Unlike the rest of Europe, to use campsites in Sweden a Camping Card Scandinavia is required. This card is not required in the rest of Scandinavia if you have a Camping Card International. Sweden does not accept the CCI and engaging the campsite staff in a lengthy discussion is pointless. The card is free and is available in advance from www.camping.se or from campsites in Sweden, but the validation stamp at your first campsite costs 90 SEK (around £7). There is a range of campsites to suit everyone. Some campsites offer a Quick Stop facility where campsite facilities can be used from 9pm to 9am, ideal for those touring the country wishing to reduce campsite costs. Some campsites are open all year.

There are few camper-stops in Sweden but www.camping-total.de/service/continent details sani stations. Free-parking is possible, especially good are the community recreational facilities normally sited by lakes and rivers throughout the country. Curiously Swedish tourist information recommends campsite use for safety and security, but provides hundreds if not thousands of walking huts. Our experience is, along with Norway, that we felt safer here than in any other country. Also the extended daylight gives added security.

Driving and Roads

The main roads in Sweden are good, though there is little dual carriageway in the north but areas are provided for overtaking. Minor roads can be extremely bumpy and pot holed. At traffic lights the Swedes tend to leave a car's length between each vehicle, which allows them to pull away all together. Driving through Sweden is regarded as the quick way to return from Nordkapp or North Norway. With few hills and no tolls it is both quick and cheap but it is also regarded as boring as there is not much to see. Moose pose a risk to motorists who are advised to slow or stop and allow the animal to move off before proceeding.

Time of year to visit

June and July is the best time to visit, preferably in a heat wave year. It is not advised to visit in the winter unless in a suitably winterised motorhome, like the Scandinavian Nordic. The North of the country is home to vast numbers of mosquitoes. Effective mosquito defences including fly screens, insect repellant, and after bite.

Tourist Information

Swedish Travel and Tourism Council, 5 Upper Montague Street, London, W1H 2AG Tel: 020 7870 5600 or visit www.visit-sweden.com . *Greater Freedom - Campsites and*

Cottages in Sweden is a tourist office publication that has some campsites and tourist information.

Things to do

Get in touch with nature, it really is worth getting off the main routes but there is little tourism outside of Stockholm. Not to be missed is the elaborate changing of the guard.

Sweden is one of the few European countries that allow virtually unlimited access to its countryside, ideal for those that love the outdoors. This allows people to walk, cycle, ride, ski and boat virtually anywhere as long as you cause no damage, respect people who live nearby, do not enter any gardens, and do not leave any rubbish. You are also allowed to pitch a tent for one night, but not too close to a home.

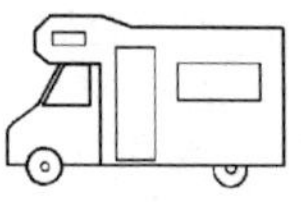

Switzerland

Clean living, fresh air and alpine beauty are images that come to mind, but there are a wealth of attractions in Switzerland. There is a melting pot of outdoor activity from the country whose national dish is fondue.

Accommodation

There are around 600 campsites. www.swisscamps.ch/GB has details of the many campsites in Switzerland. There are camper-stops in Switzerland in towns, on farms and at restaurants detailed in the *Bord Atlas* camper-stop book. The tourist information website clearly states 'Camping outside official campsites is not allowed in Switzerland'.

Driving and roads

Road tax is needed to drive in Switzerland, it is available at the border and costs around £20. Be aware that those over 3.5 tons need to pay more. Roads are good, though care should be taken on mountain passes, especially in snowy conditions.

Time of year to visit

Switzerland is an Alpine country and a year round destination. Cold and snowy in the winter and warm and sunny in Summer.

Tourist Information

Switzerland Travel Centre, 10 Wardour St, London, W10 6QF. Tel: 020 74204900 www.switzerlandtravelcentre.co.uk or www.myswitzerland.com. This country is presently outside the EU.

Things to do

Renowned for banking, chocolate and clocks Switzerland has another claim to fame, the highest concentration of museums in the world, 980 in total which may drive you cuckoo. As with most Alpine counties there is excellent skiing in Winter, with walking and mountain biking as popular Summer pastimes.

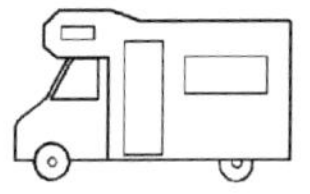

United Kingdom

There is so much to see and do that weekends and holidays can easily be filled. Unfortunately the UK is the least motorhome friendly country in Europe.

Accommodation

There is a wide network of independent campsites throughout the UK and two major clubs offer a variety of sites just about everywhere in the UK, including inside London.

The Camping and Caravan Club - is open to users of caravans, motorhomes and tents offering temporary membership for three months to foreign nationals for £10. Also available is a Freedom Pass, similar to camping cheques, for five, seven, 14 or 21 nights camping at club sites, but not certified locations. Membership gives access to all the 95 club sites and 1200 certified locations, also a copy of 'Your place in the Country' a guide to these sites. Many of the larger club sites are open to ad hoc non member visitors, who pay full rate. Some sites offer a Motorhome Service Point, where motorhomers can fill with fresh water, dump and use facilities for three hours for £4.85. Holders of CCI cards can use club sites but will not receive a copy of the guide. Annual membership costs £30 plus £5 joining fee contact the membership department on Tel: 02476 475442 or visit www.campingandcaravanclub.co.uk. Membership can also be taken out at club sites.

The Caravan Club - is open to caravanners and motorhomers. Annual membership is £32 plus £5 joining fee either visit www.caravanclub.co.uk or join at any club site. Members receive a sites' guide, discounts at club sites including Crystal Palace in London and access to the 2500 certified locations across the country.

Certified Locations (CL)- These locations are available through both clubs and are open to a maximum of five member caravans/motorhomes per night. These are located at farms, pubs and in people's gardens. They all offer water and dumping facility, some offer electricity and showers. Information of these locations are detailed in the clubs handbooks. Prices start from £3.50 per night and offer a cheap way of travelling through the UK giving access to off the beaten track or prime tourist areas. Cost of membership to one of the clubs is quickly redeemed when CL's are used. We always look to use these first whether weekending or travelling around the country. These also offer a real experience of UK culture in otherwise inaccessible areas.

camper-stops - These are a relatively new in the United Kingdom although there is growing pressure from the motorhome community to provide more facilities across the UK. Visit www.motorcaravanmagazine.co.uk to link to Stopovers UK a website detailing camper-stop facilities.

For those interested in free-parking visit www.wildcamping.co.uk and scroll down to bottom of the page. Free-parks are listed under England, Scotland and Wales and then divided into counties. These are updated by regular free-parkers and people are invited to update the site when they can. Although Ireland and Europe are listed these at present provide little or no information, also visit www.sleepingspots.co.uk. Pubs and farmers will often let you stop for the night if asked nicely, useful both in busy towns and remote areas. Normally it is possible to stop overnight at motorway service stations both with caravans and motorhomes, some require a ticket to be purchased. Unlike mainland Europe there have been no reported incidents of gas attacks in the UK. The Camping and Caravan Club *Your Big Sites Book* lists motorway service stations where it is possible to 'night halt' including location and telephone number.

Caravan or motorhome - This is surprisingly an easy question to answer, you only have to look on any campsite or drive around the suburbs to see many Brits have a caravan. If you intend to mainly holiday or tour the UK then a caravan is absolutely the best option. This is simply because of the lack of camper-stops and free-park opportunities but the thousands of cheap CL's go a long way to make up for this. The third reason is the relatively small size of the UK and the congestion on roads; once the caravan is sited a car is so much easier than a motorhome. Foreign visitors still only have one vehicle to insure, register and MOT, as caravans only need to be in a roadworthy condition and the insured car usually has third party liability for any vehicle being towed. Second hand caravans are bought and sold without any need for registration. There is a body called CRIS that claims to be the UK's official database of caravans and their keepers. They advertise having 300,000 caravans on file and all British manufactured caravans built since 1992 have been registered when first sold. CRIS can be contacted Tel: 01722 411430 to attempt to confirm legal ownership. £1000 will buy both a serviceable car and caravan.

Driving and roads

Britain has some of the busiest roads in Europe and most towns in the Southeast and Midlands suffer rush hours from 8-9am and 5-6pm and are best avoided. More rural counties suffer less. Roads are, despite local opinion, good and free to use, apart from toll bridges crossing major estuaries and the M6 toll road around Birmingham. There are a few privately owned minor toll roads in more remote areas. These are cheap and often fun to use. British drivers, on the whole, are good.

Time of year to visit

The UK is mild throughout the year and suitable for all year camping, the Winter is likely to be wet with occasional cold snaps. Scotland is best visited during the Summer, be warned mosquitoes are a problem. Realistically the UK is best toured from April to October.

Tourist Information

Contact your local tourist information or www.visitbritain.com

Things to do

As with France, Germany and Italy you can easily occupy yourself for a year, Joining the National Trust, £38 www.thenationaltrust.org.uk or English Heritage, £36 www.english-heritage.org.uk. This will provide hundreds of historic buildings and places to visit for free after membership paid, including buildings owned by the National Trust for Scotland www.nts.org.uk (if you join the National Trust). The National Trust offers free entry to members of affiliated overseas National Trusts: Australia, New Zealand, Barbados, Bermuda, Canada, Jersey, Guernsey, and Isle of Man. so bring your membership card. Don't bother to join in advance simply go to one of the more popular sites and join there.

Former Yugoslavia: Bosnia Herzegovina, Serbia and Montenegro, Kosovo, Albania

The break up of the Former Yugoslavia has left the above countries difficult for the tourist. Visitors to these countries should be aware of landmines. By staying on concreted areas and avoiding wilderness - that includes driving off the roads to Free-Park, the biggest problem of inadvertently stepping on or driving onto an unexploded landmine is avoidable.

Consult the foreign office website www.fco.gov.uk Tel: 0845 8502829 and read their detailed information on visas, licences and road conditions as well as areas to avoid. Ensure that adequate insurance and an International Driving Permit is obtained before you travel. Having said that, these countries are becoming more tourist friendly every year. Those intending to visit these countries will need to be independent and adventurous, not all have campsites of any description. Ideally a visit should take place in late spring to summer.

At the time of writing the Foreign Office advised against travel to parts of Albania. These countries are presently outside the EU.

Chapter 10 - Directory

Government Departments

DVLA, Swansea SA99 1BL Tel: 0870 2400010. www.dvla.gov.uk,

European Health Insurance Card Tel: 0845 6062030 or visit www.dh.gov.uk/travellers

Foreign and Commonwealth Office, King Charles St, London SW1A 2AH, Tel: 0845 8502829. www.fco.gov.uk

Defra, Information Recource Centre, Lower Ground Floor, Ergon House, c/o Nobel House, 17 Smith Square, London SW1P 3JR Tel:0207 238 6609 www.defra.gov.uk/animalh/quarantine/pets

Organisations

CRIS visit www.hpicheck.com or the National Caravan Council or email cris.uk@hpi.co.ukTel: 01722 411430

Motorhome Information Service, Maxwelton House, Boltro Road, Haywards Heath, West Sussex RH16 1BJ Tel: 01444 453399

National Caravan Council, Catherine House, Victoria Road, Aldershot, Hampshire GU11 1SS Tel:01252 318251 www.nationalcaravan.co.uk

Motorhome Product Companies

Action Replay, 1 The Laurels, Basingstoke, Hants Tel: 05511 436245 normal rate or www.action-replay.co.uk

Al-Ko Kober Ltd, South Warwickshire Business Park, Kineton Road, Southam, Warwickshire, CV47 0AL Tel:01926 818500 www.al-ko.co.uk

Autogas 2000 Ltd, Carlton Miniott, Thursk, North Yorkshire. YO7 4NJ Tel: 01845 523213

Axiam, AIXAM-MEGA, 56 route de Pugny, 73101 Aix les Bains Cédex www.axiam.co.uk. For a UK importer try www.axaim-cars.co.uk

Barden UK Ltd, Energy House, Segensworth East, Fareham, Hampshire PO15 5SB Tel: 01489 570770 www.barden-uk.com

BP Tel: 0845 6076943 www.bpgaslight.com

Caravan Accessories C.A.K tanks Ltd, Princes Drive Industrial Estate, Kenilworth, Warwickshire. CV8 2FD Tel: 0870 7572324 www.caktanks.co.uk

Calor Gas Ltd, Athena Drive, Tachbrook Park, Warwick CV34 6RL Tel: 0800 626626 www.calor.co.uk

Concept Edge Ltd, 12 Pield Heath Road, Hillingdon, Middlesex UB83NF Tel: 01895850455. www.conceptedge.co.uk

Dynamic Battery Services Ltd, Unit 1, Gillibrands Road, East Gillibrands Estate, Skelmersdale, Lancs WN8 9TA Tel: 01695 557575

Elecsol Europe, 47 First Avenue, Deeside Industrial Park, Deeside, Flintshire CH5 2LG Tel:0800 163298 www.elecsol.com

Fiamma visit www.Fiamma.com or your local Fiamma dealer

Gaslow International Ltd, Unit 1, Weldon Road, Loughborough, Leicestershire LE11 5RA Tel: 0870 744 6911 www.gaslow.co.uk

Globelink Language Solutions, 59 Belgrave Road, Seaford, East Sussex BN25 2HE Tel: 0871 2182008 info@globelinkone2one.com For Pass the Phone.

Michelin Tyre PLC, Campbell Road, Stoke-on-Trent ST4 4EY Tel: 01782 402000 www.michelin.com

Moore Power, Newhaven, East Sussex Tel: 01273 615348 www.moore-power.co.uk

MTH Gas Systems Limited, Castlemain Workshop, Yorkley Road, Parkend, Glos GL15 4HH Tel: 01594 563538 www.mthautogas.co.uk

Nova Leisure, 3 Mere Farm Business Complex, Redhouse Lane, Hannington, Northants, NN6 9SZ Tel:01604 780022 www.novaleisure.com

O'Leary Spares and Accessories, 314 Plaxton Bridge Road, Woodmansey, Nr Beaverley, East Yorkshire, HU17 ORS Tel: 01482 868632

PRO-Tow Frames, Unit 1, 565 Blandford Road, Hamworthy, Poole, Dorset BH16 5BW Tel: 01202 632456 www.protowframes.co.uk

PWS Engineering Ltd, Unit 5, Chalwyn Ind.Est., Old Wareham Road, Parkstone, Poole, Dorset BH12 4PE Tel: 01202 746851 www.pwsacc.co.uk

Riverway Leisure, Riverway Leisure, Chain Caul Road, Docklands, Preston PR2 2XR Tel:01772 729999 www.riverswayleisure.co.uk

Road Pro Ltd, Stephenson Close, Drayton Fields, Daventry, Northammptonshire NN11 8RF Tel: 01327 312233 www.roadpro.co.uk

SIM4travel, SIM4travel Limited, PO Box 50356, London W4 2ZA Tel: 0905 335 0336 (40p per minute) www.SIM4travel.com

Sky Tel: 08706 061111 or www.sky.com

Skype www.skype.com

Sleep-C-Cure, PO Box 35639, London SE9 2WF Tel: 01580 895358 www.Sleep-C-Cure.co.uk

Sterling Power Products Ltd www.sterling-power.com Tel: 01905 453999.

Symonspeed Ltd, Cleeveland Garage, 1 Cleeveland Road, Torquay TQ2 5BD Tel: 01803 214602 www.airide.co.uk

TB Turbo, Turbo House, Port Royal Avenue, Off Willow Lane, Lancaster LA1 5QP Tel: 01524 67157. www.turboboost.co.uk

Towsure Branches in Sheffield, Birmingham and Southampton Tel: 0870 6090070 www.towsure.com

Transleisure, Transleisure Ltd, Howley Park Ind Estate, Howley Park Road East, Morley,Leeds LS27 0BN Tel: 0113 2522900 www.Transleisure.co.uk

TVAC (Drinkwater Engineering), Centurion Way, Layland, Lancashire PR26 6TZ Tel: 01772 457116.

Unique Motor Company, Fenny Bridges, Honiton, Devon EX14 3BG Tel: 0870 2414804 www.uniquemotorcompany.co.uk

Van Bitz Motorhome Security Solutions, Cornish Farm, Shoreditch, Taunton, Somerset TA3 7BS Tel: 01823 321992 www.vanbits.com

AVC Broadband Ltd, Bessemer Drive, Stevenage, Herts SG1 2DT Tel: 0870 850 0187 www.avcbroadband.com.

Satcodx www.satcodx.com

Astra www.ses-astra.com

Dealers/manufacturers

Check motorhome magazines for details of dealers and manufacturers of motorhomes.

Travel Companies

Camping Cheque UK, Spelmonden Old Oast, Goudhurst, Kent TN17 1HE Tel: 0870 4054057 www.campingcheque.co.uk

Camping card ACSI UK, BRT/EIN/152043/UK, PO Box 66, Hounslow TW5 9RT www.camping-card.co.uk or www.campingcard.com

GB Privilege, 3 The Fields, Tacolneston, Norfolk NR16 1DG Tel: 01953 789661 www.gbprivilege.com

Perestroika Tours, Schinderhannes 1, D-56291 Hausbay, Germany Tel: Germany 06746 80280 www.mir-tours.de

TCH Holidays,9 Hexham Way, Shrewsbury SY2 6QX Tel: 01743 242354 www.tchholidays.co.uk

Touring Cheque, Hartford Manor, Greenbank Lane, Northwich, Cheshire CW8 1HW Tel:0870 9060123 www.touringcheque.co.uk

Clubs

American RV, 27 Nether End, Great Dalby, Leicestershire, LE14 2EY Tel: 08700 115111 www.arvm.uk.com

The Camping and Caravan Club, Greenfields House, Westwood Way, Coventry, CV4 8JH Tel: 02476 422024 www.campingandcaravanclub.co.uk

The Caravan Club East Grinstead, West Sussex, RH19 1BR Tel: 01342 316101 www.thecaravanclub.co.uk

Motor Caravanners Club, Freepost (TK1292), Twickenham, TW2 5BR Tel: 020 8893 3883 www.motorcaravanners.org.uk

The Motorhome Ticket Club, MTC Travel, Independence House, 25 Bolton Street, Brixham Devon, TQ5 9BZ Tel: 01803 855555 www.ferrytickets.net

Saga Services Ltd, The Saga Building, Middelburg Square, Folkestone, Kent CT20 1AZ Tel: 0800 015 6833 www.saga.co.uk

Insurance

Bakers of Cheltenham, Freepost GR1604, The Quadrangle, Imperial Square, Cheltenham, Gloucestershire, GL50 1PZ Tel:01242 528844 www.towergategroup.co.uk

British Insurance Brokers Association on Tel: 0207 623 9043 or emailing enquiries@biba.org.uk

Comfort Insurance, Comfort House, 8 Goresbrook Road, Dagenham RM9 6UR Tel: 020 8984 0777 www.comfort-insurance.co.uk

Endsleigh, Endsleigh Insurance Services Ltd, Shurdington Road, Cheltenham, Gloucestershire GL51 4UE Tel:0800 0283571 www.endsleigh.co.uk

STA Travel, visit one of the 65 branches nationwide phone for details of your nearest one or for more information Tel:08701 630026 www.statravel.co.uk

Downunder Worldwide Insurance Services, 3 Spring Street, Paddington, London W2 3RA Tel: 020 7402 9211
www.duinsure.com

Websites

www.a-motorhome-on-tour.co.uk
www.autotrader.co.uk
www.caravanning-online.co.uk
www.eurocampingcar.co.uk
www.go-overland.com
www.ideamerge.com/motoeuropa
www.jollyinteresting.co.uk
www.magbaztravels.com
www.masta.org
www.mobile.de
www.motorcaravanning.co.uk
www.motorhomefacts.com
www.motorhomeinfo.co.uk
www.motorhome-list.org.uk
www.satelliteforcaravans.co.uk
www.thewrinklies.co.uk
www.ukmotorhomes.net
www.worldofmotorhomes.com
www.xor.org.uk

Further Information

There are numerous suppliers of all things 'motorhome'. Those mentioned in this publication are simply to be used as a reference point. They are not recommendations. Those companies and products not mentioned should not deem this as negative. It is simply not possible to mention everything or every company. We therefore recommend that readers search the internet and refer to advertisements in motorhome magazines.

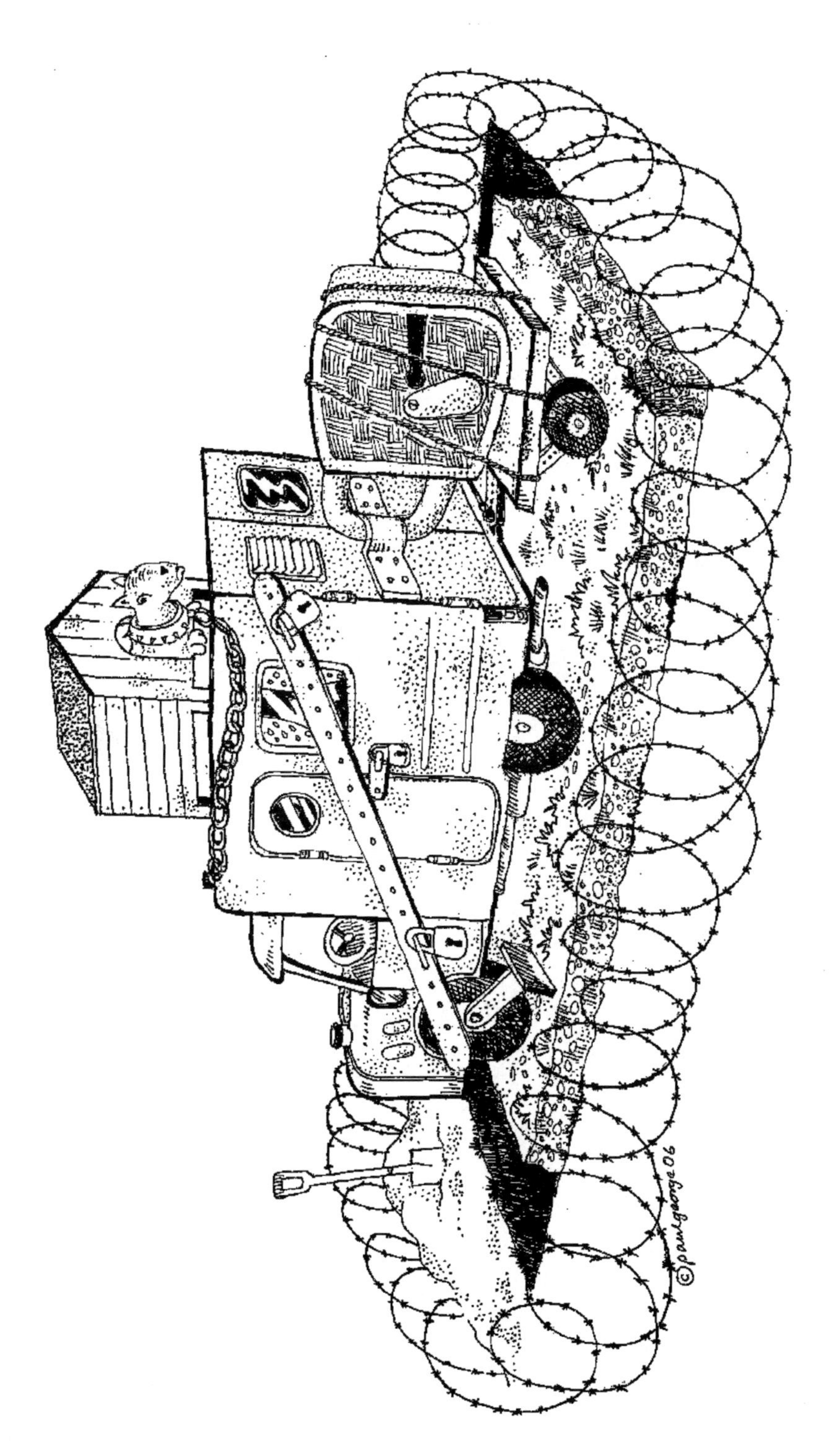